Key Regulatory Initiatives in EU Sustainable Banking

International Banking and Securities Law

Volumes published in this Brill Research Perspective are listed at *brill.com/rpbs*

Key Regulatory Initiatives in EU Sustainable Banking

Exploring Sustainability Risk Management in the EU Banking Industry

By

Alexandra-Cristina Hanganu

BRILL

LEIDEN | BOSTON

This paperback book edition is simultaneously published as issue 5.1–2 of *International Banking and Securities Law* DOI: 10.1163/24056936-12340013.

Library of Congress Control Number: 2023936702

Typeface for the Latin, Greek, and Cyrillic scripts: "Brill". See and download: brill.com/brill-typeface.

ISSN 2405-6928
ISBN 978-90-04-54318-8 (paperback)
ISBN 978-90-04-54319-5 (e-book)

This book is printed on acid-free paper and produced in a sustainable manner.

Contents

Key Regulatory Initiatives in EU Sustainable Banking

Exploring Sustainability Risk Management in the EU Banking Industry

Alexandra-Cristina Hanganu

Abstract

With temperature exhibiting a growing trend and posing threats to future generations, the Paris Agreement set a cap level of no more than 2°C for the temperature increase, emphasizing the need for cross-national participation to combat climate change. At the European level, the European Commission pledged to make Europe achieve carbon neutrality by mid-century. However, to deliver on its commitment, extensive financial support and engagement from both private and public-sector players were acknowledged as requisites. Therefore, through their funding mechanism, banks assumed a leading role in financing the transition to a green economy. Yet, a new challenge of systemic nature – i.e. ESG risks – emerged, gaining regulatory attention and subsequently triggering numerous regulatory reforms. To date, the focus at the European level rests on the development of a comprehensive definition of ESG risks as well as of a system to identify activities in scope, i.e. the EU Taxonomy that can be nonetheless assessed as the core regulatory framework on which amendments that followed were based. To address the dynamics of the regulatory landscape and to ensure compliance, banks undertook several strategic changes. Not only that they adjusted the offered products and services, but they also amended their governance structures. Specifically, a clear shift could have been identified from employing profit maximization strategies to conducting activities that serve the interests of not only shareholders but a broader category of stakeholders including the general public as well as the surrounding environment. Following the implementation of sustainability-related strategic initiatives, changes in banks' performance and their risk-taking capabilities could have been identified. Therefore, aiming to explore the extent to which ESG consideration can be considered as a strategic opportunity, or contrastingly a challenge, mixed opinions were acknowledged pointing towards the complexity of the topic at hand, complexities which are enhanced by the topic's novelty as well as by the uncertain and convoluted nature of the EU regulatory environment addressing sustainability.

 | DOI:10.1163/9789004543195_002

Keywords

ESG – EU banking industry – strategy – risk management – European sustainability-driven regulatory environment – ESG risks – EU Taxonomy – GAR – disclosure requirements

1 Introduction

Over the last decade, the global temperature increased by 1.09°C above the 1850–1900 average, from which 1.07°C are likely to have been generated as a result of activities undertaken by people (Intergovernmental Panel on Climate Change, 2021, pp. 5–6). Similarly, in accordance with the National Oceanic and Atmospheric Administration (NOAA) (2022b, n.p.), this year's April was reported as ranking in top ten warmest months of such kind since 2010, and the 448th sequential month with temperatures above the 1901–2000 average. More specifically, April 2022 recorded an increase of 0.85°C above the mean temperature characteristic for the aforementioned time window (NOAA, 2022b, n.p.). On a European level only, a temperature rise of 1.28°C above the 20th-century average occurred last year, marking an increase higher than the global average for the same year – i.e. 0.84°C – as well as an uninterrupted sequence of yearly temperature rises for the past two-and-half decades (NOAA, 2022a, n.p.). When considering the contributions people have to global warming, it is estimated that the human-driven impact was 49% greater than the 1900's benchmark value, out of which 80% was due to carbon dioxide (CO_2) (NOAA, 2022c, n.p.). With the global temperature continuously rising and posing an imminent threat to future generations, a strong need has been identified to cap this temperature rise to 1.5–2.0°C compared to pre-industrial levels, in accordance with Article 2 of the Paris Agreement (United Nations, 2015, p. 3). However, to comply with the pre-defined threshold of 1.5°C, the Intergovernmental Panel on Climate Change (2018, p. 12) estimates that global decarbonization of 45% compared to the 2010 level has to occur by 2030, followed by a net-zero level by 2050. Therefore, worldwide, a sense of urgency could have been ascertained and coordinated cross-national geopolitical participation became an absolute necessity.

On a regional level, the European Commission (EC) (2020a, n.p.) pledged to make Europe achieve carbon neutrality by mid-century and acknowledged the essential role of both private and public funding to support the transition to a green economy. Given its reduction in greenhouse gas emissions (GHG) of 24% in 2019 as opposed to the 1990 level, one could derive that Europe takes a leading position globally when it comes to sustainability (Eurostat, 2021, n.p.). However, to accelerate the process of continental decarbonization and to ensure the achievement of its ambitious targets, it was predicted that a minimum of EUR 1 trillion will be necessary for the transition by 2030, of which at least EUR 100 billion will be provided, at a European level, via the so-called *The Just Transition Mechanism* that covers the period spanning between 2021–2027 and focuses particularly on providing funds to critical areas, in addition to the contributions made from the EU budget and by means of national co-financing (EC, 2020d, n.p.). Yet, a financing gap can be recognized, highlighting one more time the essential role of various market participants in leading the economy to its sustainable future.

Banks, through their lending mechanisms, are becoming increasingly active in the field of sustainability, taking a driving seat. For example, covering the period between 2014–2021, the Climate Bonds Initiative (2022, n.p.) reported that 22% of the cumulative dollar amount of green bonds was issued by financial institutions, ranking second and being placed in the immediate proximity of non-financial corporations which issued 23% of that cumulative amount. Likewise, Newton, Ongena, Xie, and Zhao (2022, p. 18) assess the role played by both capital markets and banks in financing the transition to a green economy and emphasize financial institutions' efficiency in this regard. Specifically, any negative environmental, social, and governance (ESG) surprises experienced by a borrower might determine banks to disrupt their lending relationship with the respective debtor, indirectly exercising pressure on the latter to deliver on its sustainability commitments (Newton et al., 2022, p. 18). Thus, financial institutions operating in the European Union (EU) will represent the subject of this research. While the focus rests on credit institutions only, due to the existing interconnectedness between the various financial market participants, caution should be exercised when considering the findings presented in this paper, and additionally, further research conducted about any externalities and/or implications derived from banks' sustainability-related initiatives onto other financial market participants such as, for example, insurance companies.

While sustainable finance is recognized to positively contribute to the EC green agenda, new challenges emerged for market participants, known as environmental, social and governance risks. Particularly in the banking industry, ESG risks can be classified as transition risks including elements like policy and regulation, technology development and customer preferences, or physical risks – risks directly related to environmental changes (Network for Greening the Financial System, 2021, p. 10). It follows that, through economic transition channels, climate risks result ultimately in financial risks with a potential systemic impact (NGFS, 2021, p. 10).

Given the systemically important nature of ESG risks, the regulatory and supervisory environment is constantly changing, generating conflicting attitudes. On the one hand, regulators attempt to take early action. For example, the European

Banking Authority (EBA) (2019, p. 6) aims to amend the *Capital Requirements Regulation* (CRR II) and the *Capital Requirements Directive* (CRD V). These amendments imply the identification and delineation of ESG risks, as well as the establishment of measures to comprehend the effects ESG risks can have over different time horizons, of strategies and mechanisms through which credit institutions can address such risks, and of analysis methods for assessing ESG risks' impact on banks' activities (EBA, 2019, p. 6). On the other hand, academia is rather reluctant toward the efficiency and effectiveness of current regulatory frameworks addressing sustainability. Increases in capital requirements can be counterproductive, leading to a growing cost of financing for credit institutions due to the low-risk anomaly of banks' stocks (Baker & Wurgler, 2015, pp. 318–319). Additionally, capital requirements regulatory frameworks do not distinguish between environmentally friendly projects and brown investments (Gursoy, 2016, p. 72). Thus, they do not represent any incentive mechanism for banks to involve in green financing (Gursoy, 2016, p. 72). It can be derived thus that, in order to address the complex nature of the current regulatory environment, the competent authorities should take into consideration and address the identified limitations before developing and introducing further regulatory frameworks.

To date, the focus of regulatory reforms has been oriented towards primarily developing a comprehensive understanding of ESG risks, with a strong emphasis being placed on climate risks, and on establishing harmonized disclosure requirements. Specifically, at the European level, the European Commission (EC) (2020d, n.p.) introduced in July 2020 the *EU Taxonomy – Regulation (EU) 2020/852 of the European Parliament and of the Council of 18 June 2020 on the establishment of a framework to facilitate sustainable investment* – which consists of both the general characteristic of activities supporting sustainability goals, as well as a concrete list of such cross-industrial activities. The EU Taxonomy has been further complemented by EBA's proposal to the EC for developing a *Green Asset Ratio* (GAR) which computes the amount of funding banks direct toward environmentally friendly investments compliant with the EU Taxonomy (EBA, 2021a, n.p.). With EBA having a mandate by 2023 to assess the prudential treatment of ESG risks as well as their inclusion into ESG risk-management frameworks and into stress-testing exercises, a recalibration of this research paper was needed, and a focus shift occurred from evaluating European ESG risk-management frameworks to consider the impact of regulatory initiatives addressing ESG risks from a more qualitative, strategy-oriented perspective. However, according to Ben-Amar, Boujenoui, and Zéghal (2014, p. 16), a company's strategy and its risk-management approach are interlinked, where the former ultimately determines the employed risk management strategy given the various risk exposure levels implied by varying strategic options available to companies.

To address the dynamics of the regulatory landscape and to ensure compliance, credit institutions undertook several strategic changes. Specifically, banks contribute to the green transition not only through financing sustainability-compliant investments but also through various other activities such as encouraging the utilization of public transportation or using green energy for their physical subsidiaries (Zimmermann, 2019, p. 2267). Additionally, a change appears to have taken place in terms of banks' governance structures. Precisely, a shift occurred from the "*shareholder theory*" which advocates for strategies maximizing shareholders' returns only, to the "*stakeholder theory*" which supports the implementation of strategies serving the interest of a broader category of stakeholders, including the general public (Miralles-Quirós, Miralles-Quirós, & Hernández, 2019, p. 1405). Focusing particularly on the Board's structure and its female representation, Birindelli, Dell' Atti, Iannuzzi, and Savioli (2018, p. 4714) assert that a balance between the number of male and female Board members tends to be positively correlated with the performance of a credit institution, supporting thus only partially the "*dual critical mass*" theory. However, Nosratabadi, Pinter, Mosavi, and Semperger (2020, p. 2328) stress the challenging nature of establishing and employing a sustainable business model which can address both ESG issues and generate expected shareholder returns. Consequently, in the absence of regulatory incentives, despite sustainability-driven initiatives having been implemented, industry practitioners find it rather challenging to pursue strategies that are not short-term profitable and to accelerate their efforts to supporting the transition to a green economy.

Given that ESG and sustainable finance became salient topics in the banking industry, several quantitative studies were conducted, testing the relationship between ESG performance and banks' profitability or their risk-taking appetite/capabilities. Examples of such studies recently published include Azmi, Hassan, Houston, and Karim (2021), Chiaramonte, Dreassi, Girardone, and Piserà (2021), as well as Buallay, Fadel, Alajmi, and Saudagaran (2021). Yet, as the number of studies increased, so did the contradictory opinions among academia. One body of research acknowledged the opportunities resulting from sustainability-driven corporate strategies. Specifically, it was recognized in the existing literature that corporate strategies supporting sustainability can lead to reductions in the cost of capital, as well as to sustainable long-term corporate profitability (La Torre, Leo, & Panetta, 2021, p. 1621). Furthermore,

Chiaramonte et al. (2021, p. 1200) identified that banks' stability during crisis – as indicated by the distance to default – is positively correlated to ESG scores, pointing towards prudent bank activities and reputational enhancement via improved stakeholder relationships.

Conversely, another body of research deems the inclusion of ESG considerations in corporate activities and processes as a strategic burden. Buallay et al. (2021, p. 758) highlight the negative correlation between ESG scores and banks' performance, regardless of the place of incorporation, i.e. developed or developing countries. Focusing on risk-taking and banks' value, Di Tommaso and Thornton (2020, pp. 2292–2293) emphasize the presence of a trade-off. Namely, while ESG investments improve banks' crisis resilience, the bank's value is reduced due to resources being committed to investments that are not short-term profitable (Di Tommaso & Thornton, 2020, pp. 2292–2293). Azmi et al. (2021, p. 16) stress the extent to which ESG activities performed by banks exhibit a diminishing return-to-scale trend once a certain threshold is reached.

As opposed to previous studies that address sustainability from a quantitative perspective only, the purpose of this study is to explore and provide a comprehensive overview of the current European regulatory environment addressing sustainability from a qualitative strategy-oriented risk management perspective, evaluating to what extent current regulatory frameworks can be perceived as a strategic opportunity or, contrastingly, a strategic challenge for financial institutions, which represents thus the central phenomenon of the research at hand. To be more specific, this study, structured as a literature review and qualitative content analysis, will contribute to this field of expertise by outlaying and critically assessing key European banking regulatory frameworks focused on ESG risks and, more precisely, on climate risks, after having gauged the environmental challenges that triggered geopolitical as well as regulatory measures. In this context, ESG risks are defined as any potential negative impacts generated by ESG factors on credit institutions related either to banks' own activities or to those activities undertaken by its customers, and which nevertheless result in financial risks with a potential systemically important nature (EBA, 2021b, p. 34). Following this, the effects of regulatory stimuli will be presented by highlighting the various strategic directions undertaken by credit institutions to comply with sustainability-related regulatory frameworks. Last but not least, existing quantitative papers evaluating the relationship between ESG considerations and banks' performance across various dimensions will be presented. Hence, this study will address the identified knowledge gap by drawing attention to the complexities implied by a continuously emerging topic as sustainability represents, highlighting the various existent contradictory opinions and deriving areas where further research is deemed necessary. Consequently, to serve the purpose of this study, the following central research question and sub-questions are to be answered:

What are the perceived strategic implications derived from European sustainability risk management regulatory frameworks for credit institutions?

- What are the core European regulatory initiatives designed to support the transition to a sustainable, green economy?
- What are the perceived implications of incorporating sustainability risk factors into capital requirements regulations?
- What strategies are employed by credit institutions as a response to newly introduced sustainability risk management regulatory frameworks?
- How can compliance with European sustainability risk management regulatory frameworks be perceived from a performance standpoint?

It is expected that this study could be of interest to various parties including regulators who are to be provided with a perspective on potential areas of improvement to increase frameworks' applicability in the context of current market realities. Additionally, this study is expected to be of relevance to banks' executive personnel, risk managers, as well as strategy employees at a managerial level who will be offered an overview of the most quoted strategic directions undertaken by financial institutions in complying with current ESG regulatory considerations. Nevertheless, for academia, the acknowledged limitations of this study will highlight further areas for research having the potential to bridge the knowledge gap. Lastly, this study can serve a broader audience which, in a more general sense, consists of all interested in grasping the current European sustainability-related regulatory regime.

To this end, this work will be structured as follows: Section 2 will outline the methodology selected for conducting the study as well as the developed conceptual framework utilized to guide the research at hand. In Section 3, a primary focus will be placed on the current environmental conditions considered as determinants for a strong need to implement ESG aspects on a cross-industry basis, as well as on the role played by financial institutions in supporting the transition to a green, sustainable economy. Following this, the current regulatory landscape addressing sustainability will be analyzed in Section 4. Likewise, the concept of ESG risks as defined from a regulatory perspective is to be introduced in the subsequent section. While Section 6 will emphasize how the banking industry has been adapted to reflect ESG consideration, Section 7 will analyze to what extent sustainability strategies provide opportunities or, contrastingly, challenges to financial institutions by exploring topic-related quantitative studies. Lastly, while Section 8 will summarize the findings of this contribution, Section 9 provides the concluding remarks.

2 Methodology and Conceptual Framework

Addressing the limitations identified in the existing literature on the explored topic, and aiming to develop a better understanding of the central phenomenon, i.e. the strategic impact on banks of the European sustainability regulatory environment targeted toward credit institutions, this research paper[1] is designed as a literature review. To be more specific, this study will first explore, understand, and critically assess existing European ESG regulatory frameworks such as "*EBA Report on Management and Supervision of ESG Risks for Credit Institutions and Investment Firms*" and other topic-related academic literature to identify potential areas of improvement, as well as the existing strategies employed by banks to address sustainability, documented by academia. Likewise, a series of peer-reviewed articles published in academic journals such as *Sustainability* (*Switzerland*), *The European Journal of Finance*, or *Corporate Social Responsibility and Environmental Management* will be included to primarily emphasize the complexity of the topic at hand by highlighting the contradictory opinions of researchers regarding the impact of ESG strategic directions on banks' performance. The type of data used is structured texts, including regulatory frameworks, as well as academic literature. Therefore, this work exhibits nonetheless the characteristic of a qualitative content analysis, which can be defined as the method employed to better comprehend a certain phenomenon via documents and text analysis (Bryman & Bell, 2011, p. 291).

The following reasons justify the suitability of applying the mentioned study strategy for researching the topic at hand. Firstly, given the contemporaneous and ongoing adjusting nature of sustainability, this topic tends to lack theories that attempt to explain the implementation of ESG factors in banks' strategies. However, there are certain theories that, despite their application in a different field of study, might facilitate the understanding of the topic and thus will be used to guide this research. Nevertheless, several quantitative papers aimed to establish the relationship between various ESG parameters and their impacts on banks' performance, as well as their risk-taking appetite. As supported by Bailey and Caprotti, (2014, p. 1797) sustainability and, more specifically, establishing a green economy are concepts that cannot be fully comprehended by applying only one of the following two methodologies, i.e. empirical research or existent theoretical frameworks – this topic tends to be a social-construct that rests within a complex relationship between people and the surrounding environment, requesting for an interdisciplinary view and a mix of various methodological approaches. Therefore, both cross-topic existing

1 This work represents a part of the Master Thesis published on July 4th, 2022, at Lauder Business School, Hofzeile 18–20, 1190 Vienna, Austria.

theories and previous quantitative studies were used to develop a conceptual framework that will steer this work and facilitate the process of answering the central research question, i.e. *What are the perceived strategic implications derived from European sustainability risk management regulatory frameworks for credit institutions?* Figure 1 depicts the previously mentioned conceptual framework, consisting of five elements with a causal link which will be detailed in the sections to follow.

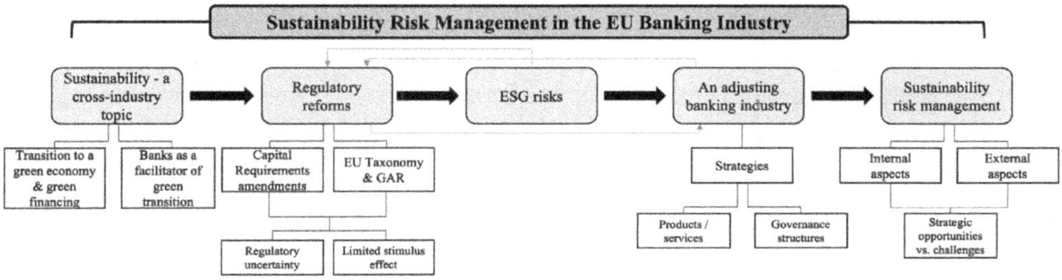

FIGURE 1 Conceptual framework: Sustainability risk management in the EU banking industry. The graph above depicts the developed conceptual framework used to guide the research at hand, consisting of five elements with a causal link.
SELF-CREATED FIGURE BASED ON THE CONDUCTED LITERATURE REVIEW

Secondly, a relationship exists between regulatory frameworks and the behavior of market participants. While the former attempts to influence the latter, the operationalization of new regulatory frameworks by market participants will lead to the identification of potential shortcomings which will trigger subsequently regulatory adjustments. For example, capital requirements regulations, and financial regulations in general, have been introduced to limit banks' risk-taking ability and to safeguard financial systems' soundness (Llewellyn, 1999, p. 9). However, with the ESG risks generated by banks' own activities and/or by their customers' activities representing new challenges to the financial system, a need emerged to adjust the existing capital requirements regulatory frameworks to address these ESG risks (EBA, 2019, p. 6). Therefore, obtaining a better understanding of the current sustainability-related regulatory environment is of utmost importance in determining the potential future directions the banking industry might undergo.

The focus of this research paper rests on the banking industry in Europe. While global initiatives and governmental programs employed to support sustainability vary, a certain level of uniformity exists at the European level. Through European Commission's commitment to achieving carbon neutrality in Europe by mid-century, pressure is exerted cross-industry for reaching such an ambitious goal and specifically on the banking industry given its financing function (EC, 2020c, n.p.). Additionally, as highlighted by Ahlström (2019,

p. 516), the interconnectedness of the European financial market law and the EU Single Market provides the necessary legal infrastructure to support the implementation of EU sustainable financing initiatives. Likewise, the EC, through its Green Deal, created a common goal for participating countries. Yet, each country has been allowed the discretion of choosing locally the mechanisms through which the common goal can be achieved, as reflected by the voluntary nature of current regulatory frameworks, as well as by the different ESG-related strategies employed by banks (Ahlström, 2019, p. 450; Zimmermann, 2019, p. 2268). Consequently, as opposed to researching credit institutions in one country only, this study examines the sustainability-related regulatory landscape at the European level.

Lastly, regarding the data analysis strategy performed, regulatory frameworks and academic literature were critically assessed to understand the central phenomenon and to identify potential shortcomings of current regulatory frameworks, as well as contradictory attitudes regarding whether the current regulatory landscape addressing sustainability can be perceived as a strategic opportunity or, contrastingly, a burden for financial institutions operating in Europe. Concise critical notes were written to summarize and analyze the researched documents and texts which were then structured in accordance with the developed conceptual framework to form the narrative of this study that is presented in the following sections.

3 Sustainability – a Cross-Industry Salient Topic

Climate change has been a concerning topic across nations for the past decades and represents a key driver for various industry and regulatory transformations, spanning from a need for mutual, cross-regional, and cross-industry involvement to ensure the well-being of future generations to come. United Nations (UN) (2021, n.p.) defines climate change as being manifested not only by increases in temperature – known as global warming – but also through various extreme climate conditions, where the former characteristic tends to be the most influential and quoted one. While solar cycles can be considered a natural cause of climatological developments, human-performed activities have been further acknowledged as meaningfully contributing to heating the surface of the planet (UN, 2021, n.p.). For these reasons, numerous geopolitical measures have been designed and implemented to firstly raise awareness of the prevailing threat planet Earth and its inhabitants are confronted with, and secondly to call for nationwide cooperation to combat the aforementioned danger and its underlining implications. Consequently, the first element of the conceptual framework mentioned in the previous section is represented by sustainability as a cross-industry salient topic. Thus, the remainder of this section details the environmental and human determinants for political reforms, outlining subsequently the major measures of such kind implemented in Europe, concluding with the role financial markets, and particularly credit institutions, play in facilitating the transition to a sustainable future.

Global temperatures have been progressively rising for successive years now. NOAA (2022a, n.p.) reports that 2021 was the 6th warmest year in a sequence of more than four decades of temperature increases, scoring heights of +0.84°C above the mean temperature for the timeframe covering the years between 1901–2000. As Figure 2 below indicates, an accelerated increase in temperature occurred starting in 1981 at a 10-years average rate of +0.18°C (NOAA, 2022a, n.p.). By contrast, at a pre-industrial level, the rate of temperature increase per decade was on average +0.08°C (NOAA, 2022a, n.p.). Earlier studies such as the one conducted in 2012 by the Organization for Economic Co-operation and Development (OECD) (2021, n.p.) indicate that the global temperature can achieve heights of 6°C above the pre-industrial level over the upcoming decades leading to the year 2100 if no sense of urgency is acknowledged nor immediate actions are undertaken. More recent studies however cap the temperature rise to 2100 at between 2.4–2.8°C given the contemporary policies in place (International Energy Agency, 2021, p. 35), or to 3.3–5.7°C respectively for the 2081–2100 period if CO_2 emissions are maintained at levels slightly above

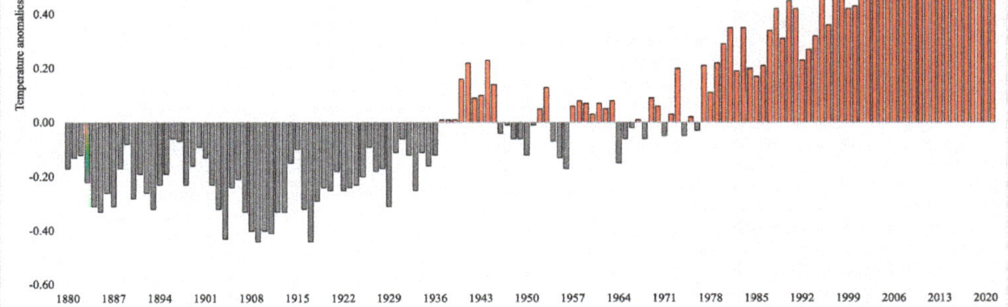

FIGURE 2 Global land and ocean January–December temperature anomalies (1880–2021). The graph above depicts the global temperature changes against the 20th century (1901–2000) average to December 2021, where 2021 was reported as the 6th warmest year with above-average temperature heights of 0.84°C (1.51°F).
NOAA, 2022A, N.P.

120 gigatons/year, highlighting thus an existing threat that has not been contained (IPCC, 2021, pp. 17–18).

The human-driven contributions to climate change via their engagement in carbon-intensive activities have been unquestionable. To be more specific, Gaffney and Steffen (2017, p. 56) highlighted that the CO_2 produced by activities people conduct on a daily basis is 100 times higher than the amount created naturally during the Ice Age, where CO_2 emissions are the primary contributor to Earth's surface heating process. Likewise, IPCC (2021, pp. 5–6) estimates that approximately 98% of the additional temperature increase last decade over the 1850–1900 average is generated by the planet's inhabitants. Additionally, NOAA (2022c, n.p.) computes an annual greenhouse gas index which calculates the radiative impact of human actions on the planet's heating process and established that, in 2021, an increase of 49% over the 1990 benchmark level occurred, of which 80% was due to CO_2 emissions only. Figure 3 depicts the previously mentioned human-driven impact, which features a growing trend and advocates for immediate remedial actions. Consequently, to maintain the temperature escalation at the level universally agreed of below 2°C, IPCC (2018, p. 12) estimates that global GHG emissions need to reach a zero level in 2050 since the temperature stabilization process requires approximately 20–30 years to materialize.

While climate change occurs to a different degree across the globe, it is Europe that tends to take a leading position in facilitating the sustainability transformation. Namely, a 24% drop in GHG emissions was reported by Eurostat

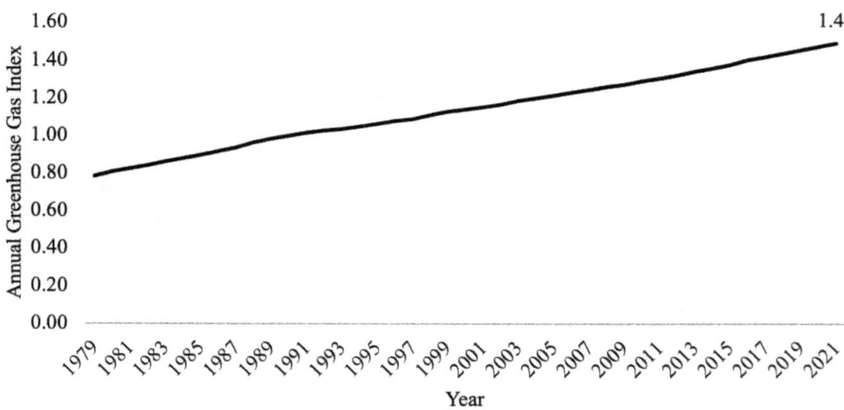

FIGURE 3 Annual Greenhouse Gas Index (AGGI).
The graph above depicts the Annual Greenhouse Gas Index, which measures the human-driven contributions to global warming on a yearly basis indexed by the 1900 year – in 2021, AGGI had a 49% increase over the 1900 benchmark.
NOAA, 2022C, N.P.

(2021, n.p.) compared to the 1990 level. As Figure 4 exhibits, on average, Europe experienced a declining trend in its produced emissions (Eurostat, 2021, n.p.). Yet, the continent has not been safeguarded against extreme climatological events and temperature increases, as well as from their financial and non-financial consequences. Specifically, it was identified that, in 2018, the mortality rate due to heat in Europe financially impacted the region by an amount equivalent to the income earned on average by 11 million citizens (Watts et al., 2021, p. 156). Likewise, NOAA (2022a, n.p) reported year 2021, with temperatures of 1.28°C above the 21st century, as being the 9th warmest year. World Health Organization (WHO) (2019, p. 5) estimated that floods occurring over the past three decades generated a cost of more than EUR 72 billion and are expected to continue affecting 300,000 and 390,000 people annually by 2050 and 2080 respectively if mitigation measures are delayed. Further concerning statistics that drive the imperative need for change were made by the EC (2021, n.p.) which assessed an increase of CO_2 atmospheric concentration above the 1750 level of 48%.

To combat climate change and to ensure the comfort, health, and safety of future generations, several geopolitical measures have been implemented across the globe. To be more specific, in 2015, the *Paris Agreement* calls for immediate action and cooperation across nations, stressing the need to cap the temperature increase to below 1.5–2°C compared to pre-industrial levels (UN, 2015, p. 3). The same Article 2 which elaborates on the decided-upon maximum temperature level additionally evokes making climate resilience a goal for participating nations, which are nevertheless required to set mechanisms allowing the efficient allocation of capital to activities that support the transition to a sustainable future (UN, 2015, p. 3). As estimated by the UN (2021, n.p.), USD 100 billion will be necessary to be invested yearly, particularly in

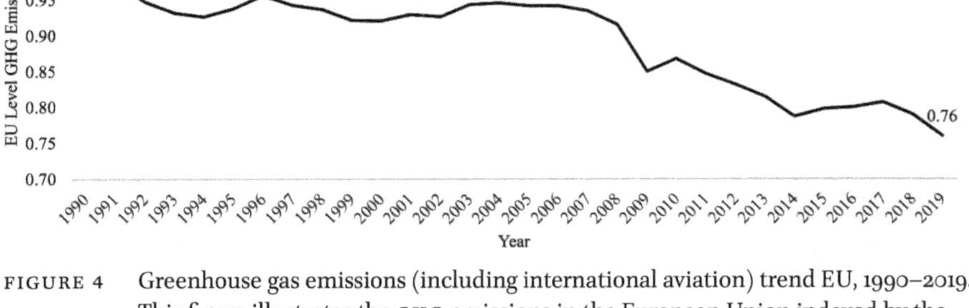

FIGURE 4 Greenhouse gas emissions (including international aviation) trend EU, 1990–2019. This figure illustrates the GHG emissions in the European Union indexed by the 1900's value – as indicated, a decline in GHG emissions of 24% relative to the chosen base year was reported in 2019.
EUROSTAT, 2021, N.P.

developing countries. While the financing needs are sizeable, the World Bank Group (2019, p. 7) expects the foreseen USD 1.8 trillion to be committed to sustainability investments for a decade between 2020–2030 to yield a USD 7.1 trillion in return. Previously, covering the same 10-year timeframe, The Global Commission on the Economy and Climate (2018, p. 8) computed a gain of USD 26 trillion if sustainability-compliant actions are implemented by various actors across industries as opposed to having them conducting activities on a business-as-usual mode. Subsequently, quoting the numbers mentioned previously both in terms of negative impacts of climate change and potential profitability opportunities by transitioning to ESG-driven business models, market players across industries should be incentivized to readjust their strategic directions, considering a long-term timeframe as part of their planning process and implementing sustainability-related initiatives in line with the goals established by the Paris Agreement and other complementary national/regional GHG emission reduction objectives.

In Europe, delivering on its commitment to the Paris Agreement as a participating party, the EC (2020a, n.p.) pledged to make the region the first climate-neutral continent across the globe, as part of the so-called *European Green Deal* presented in December 2019. According to the previously mentioned Green Deal, European-wide GHG emissions are to be reduced by 55% by 2030, reaching a net-zero level by mid-century (EC, 2020a, n.p.). Subsequently,

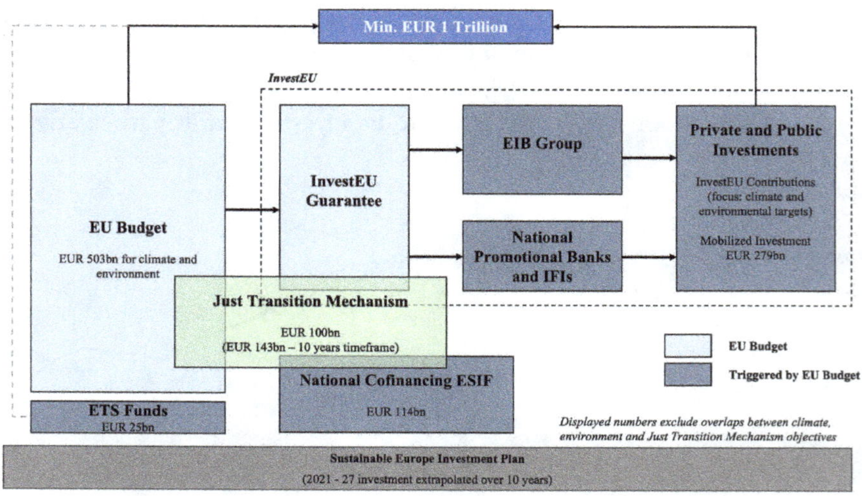

FIGURE 5 Funding elements of the European Green Deal Investment Plan. EUR 1 trillion is to be invested at the European level as part of the European Green Deal Investment Plan published in January 2020, spanning from various sources.
EC, 2020B, P. 5

in order to deliver on these ambitious goals, an investment plan was established one month after the announcement of the European Green Deal, i.e. the *European Green Deal Investment Plan*, which determines the amount to be invested for supporting the transition to a green economy, and the respective sources of financing (EC, 2020a, n.p.).

As depicted in Figure 5 above, various funding providers will be mobilized for the green transformation, collecting a total minimum amount of EUR 1 trillion for a 10-year timeframe between 2021–2030 (EC, 2020b, p. 5). The EU is expected to supply 25% of its budget for the period, i.e. EUR 503 billion, to finance the climate and environmental transition, out of which slightly more than half will be accumulated via the *InvestEU* program, calling for assistance from both the private and public sectors (EC, 2020b, p. 6). Further capital will be as well collected by means of national co-financing and via the *Innovation and Modernization Funds* – 11.4% and 0.25% respectively of the total value – where the latter source streams from the income collected under the *Emissions Trading Scheme* (EC, 2020b, p. 6). According to the *Just Transition Mechanism*, regions where carbon-intensive activities such as the exploitation of fossil fuels are prevailing and which, nevertheless, are in need of considerable restructuring will be prioritized (EC, 2020b, p. 17).

Given the necessary funding mentioned throughout the previous paragraphs, financial markets tend to assume a leading position in supporting the transition to a green sustainable economy through their funding mechanisms, a role recognized not only at the EU level, but also globally (EC, 2020a, n.p.). Specifically, in 2020, the amount of global sustainable investments increased by 15% compared to 2018, reaching USD 35.3 trillion and being the equivalent of more than a third of the total assets under management (Global Sustainable Investment Alliance, 2021, p. 9). When considering the global market for green bonds, in 2021, the dollar amount of issued green bonds increased by 71% compared to the previous year, reaching approximately USD 509 billion (Climate Bonds Initiatives, 2022, n.p.). Europe contributed 52% to reach the aforementioned half-trillion amount of issued green bonds, ranking first, followed by Asia-Pacific and North America with 25% and 18% respectively – Figure 6 (Climate Bonds Initiatives, 2022, n.p.). One more time, the figures stress the leading role Europe takes in transitioning to a green economy.

Banks, as one of the primary financial market participants, are becoming increasingly active in the field of sustainability and their role in financing the transition to a green economy has been recognized by academia. Figure 7, plotting the percentage of green bonds' cumulative issued amount for the period 2014–2021, ranks financial institutions in the second place, immediately after the non-financial corporates, with 22% (Climate Bonds Initiative, 2022, n.p.).

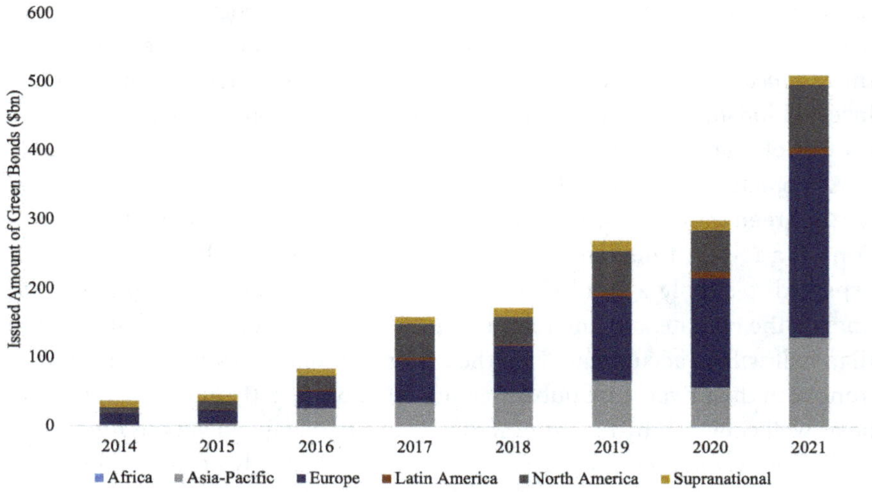

FIGURE 6 Global issued amount of green bonds (USD bn).
The graph above plots the global USD amount of green bonds issued between 2014–2021 – as indicated, Europe ranks first with approximately USD 265 billion in 2021.
CLIMATE BONDS INITIATIVE, 2022, N.P.

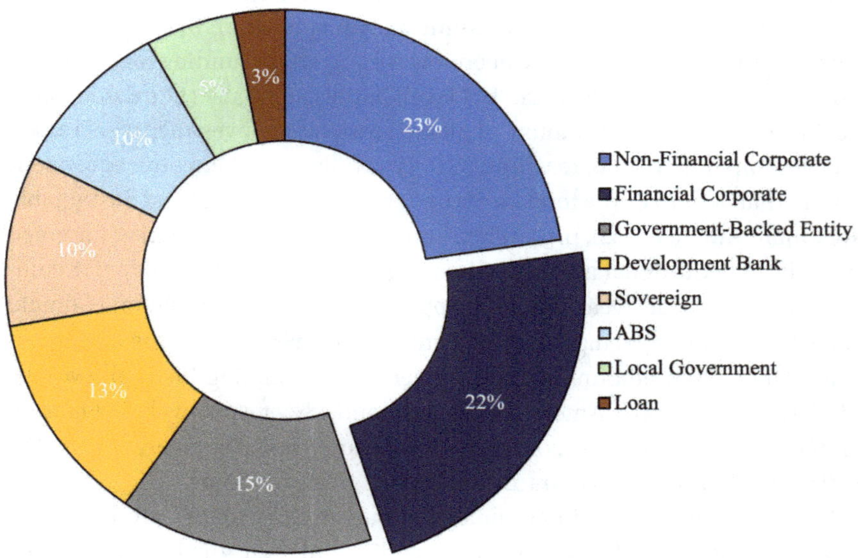

FIGURE 7 Percentage of the cumulative issued amount of green bonds by issuing mechanism.
The percentage of the cumulative amount of issued green bonds for the timeframe covering the period between 2014–2021 has been plotted above – 22% of the cumulative amount for the period was issued by financial institutions, indicating the essential role they play in the green transition.
CLIMATE BONDS INITIATIVE, 2022, N.P.

There are several arguments that support the leading role of banks in the green transformation. According to Park and Kim (2020, p. 15) banks, through their ability to redirect the capital flow to sustainability projects in need of financing, are in the position to facilitate the economy's green transformation by including ESG consideration in the assessment of current and prospective borrowers. Through a pricing mechanism where the ESG performance of corporates is valued as part of the lending cost, Eliwa, Aboud, and Saleh (2021, p. 17) reorganized that banks at the EU level significantly contribute to encouraging companies' sustainable changes by reducing the cost of debt for borrowers who implement sustainability-driven business models. However, the authors criticized the lack of differentiation between ESG performance and disclosure since they tend to be used as substitutes when valued as part of the cost of debt, a practice that might result in different real impacts on the transition and the achievement of nationwide sustainability goals. Newton et al. (2022, p. 12), in a study conducted on 3,783 publicly traded companies in the United States (US), identified a negative correlation between banks' green lending and firms' ESG risks. More specifically, banks take a competitive advantage over capital markets in that they can better screen borrowers' performance, and any ESG negative news related to a debtor might determine banks to terminate the borrower-lender relationship (Newton et al., 2022, p. 18). While companies can return to capital markets for funding to avoid the strict monitoring performed by financial institutions, Newton et al. (2022, p. 18) recognize the efficient role of banks over capital markets in motivating corporate sustainability-compliant behavior to avoid potentially disrupted lending relationships. Apart from their contribution via financing green investments and projects, credit institutions implemented other strategy-related initiatives internally to support both the reduction of their own GHG emissions and their transition to a sustainable ESG-driven business model. Those initiatives are further documented in Section 6.

As a reaction to climate change, numerous geopolitical measures have been implemented on both regional and supranational or global levels. Given the estimated financing needs to ensure the transition to a green economy, the involvement of several parties across industries is of utmost importance. Therefore, financial markets took a leading position in steering the capital flow toward sustainable-compliant investments, where banks have been recognized as one of the most efficient market players in supporting the green development. However, climate change did not trigger geopolitical measures only, but also changes in the regulatory landscape for those in need of and, equally important, for providers of capital. Consequently, the next section will be focused on regulatory reforms designed to address challenges imposed by ESG.

4 Regulatory Reforms Addressing Sustainability

Regulatory frameworks have been put in place not only to facilitate and encourage but also to enforce the transition to a green economy. As asserted in an early paper by Llewellyn (1999, p. 9), financial regulation has several economic rationales, including addressing and ensuring the stability of the financial system and of the overall economy, correcting market failures and imperfections, as well as protecting market participants against any moral hazard or adverse selection while consequently building customer confidence. Therefore, it could be derived that financial regulation attempts at changing behaviors and could be considered one of the mechanisms through which a green economy can be achieved (Ahlström, 2019, p. 450). Similarly, Raworth (2017, p. 49) developed a framework that emphasizes the connection between planetary health and social well-being, where the latter is highly dependent on the former, calling for regulatory interventions. Therefore, to accelerate the transition to a sustainable future and to address any challenges occurring along the path such as the ESG risks, regulatory bodies developed several regulatory initiatives which adjusted nonetheless the banking landscape. Subsequently, the remaining of this section will detail some of the most quoted regulatory initiatives addressing sustainability, highlighting identified limitations that pose challenges to affected financial institutions.

At an international level, the Bank for International Settlements (BIS), acting as a bank for central banks, aims at ensuring financial stability by means of global cooperation (BIS, 2005, n.p.). To deliver on its mission statement, BIS, through its Basel Committee on Bank Supervision, put in place the so-called *Basel Framework* that establishes a set of standards for banks' prudential regulation, being applied across jurisdictions and enacted for the first time as Basel I in 1992, then substituted subsequently by Basel II in 2004 (BIS, 2019, n.p.). In the aftermath of the financial crises of 2007–2008, Basel III Framework was developed, amending the previous version by strengthening the macroprudential regulation and supervision (BIS, 2017, n.p.). With the Basel Framework, a system of three pillars has been put in place addressing banks' minimum capital requirements to withstand market shocks, their risk management frameworks, as well as their disclosure requirements (BIS, 2017, n.p.). Figure 8 below depicts the structure of the Basel III Framework according to the previously mentioned pillars.

With ESG risks becoming potentially an additional category of risk that can cause financial instability, the University of Cambridge Institute for Sustainability Leadership (2014, p. 15) assessed the degree to which Basel II and Basel III

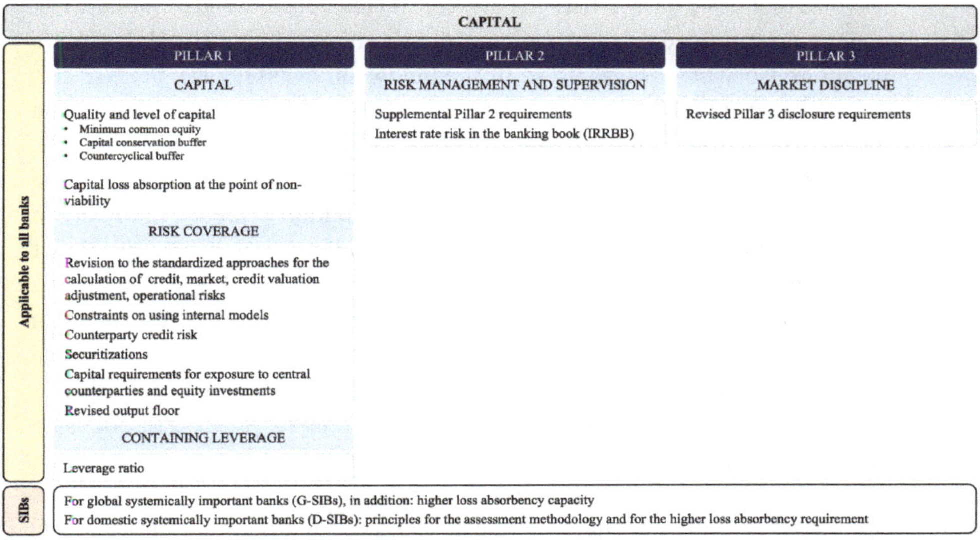

FIGURE 8 Basel III Framework consists of three pillars developed to increase the ability of banks to withstand shocks and to properly address the various systemically important risks faced by means of capital reserves, risk management frameworks, and disclosure.
BIS, 2017, N.P.

respectively address the current market challenges derived from the sustainability transition and identified that only limited consideration has been allocated to ESG risks in the mentioned frameworks. Specifically, it was acknowledged that ESG risks inclusion in the Basel II Framework is limited to Pillar I where banks are required to assess borrowers' environmental risks as part of the lending process with respect to borrowers' liability for the collateral, i.e. "deep-pockets" doctrine and the responsibility born by borrowers towards any environmental damages brought by the property or project for which funding was requested including, for example, the presence of toxic materials on the property (University of Cambridge Institute for Sustainability Leadership, 2014, p. 15). Consequently, given the systemic nature of ESG risks, a need has been recognized for amending the Basel Framework in place to better reflect this new challenge faced by industry practitioners.

Correspondingly, the initial steps have been taken by the Basel Committee as early as the last quarter of 2021 when they issued a consultation paper on the topic of suitable approaches for including environmental risks in banks' management and supervision process (BIS, 2021, n.p.). A few months later, i.e. June 2022, the Basel Committee published 18 Principles that address climate risks on a high-level basis, where the first 12 Principles are focused on climate risk management procedures for banks, while the remaining 6 Principles guide the supervisory process, as listed in the below Table (BIS, 2022, p. 1). To this end, addressing banks' corporate governance, Principles 1–3 recommend the following: the proper understating and assessment of climate risks across various time horizons and subsequently their inclusion in banks' strategies and risk-management processes, the effective participation of board members in delegating the climate-risk assessment responsibility to dedicated groups of employees and their continuous oversight over task-delivery, as well as the development and implementation of policies, procedures, and controls on a cross-divisional basis (BIS, 2022, pp. 2–3). Principle 4 emphasizes the need of incorporating sound internal control systems which can effectively identify, measure, and mitigate climate risks of material nature (BIS, 2022, p. 4). Focusing on the soundness of banks' financial stability, as part of Principle 5, climate risks are recommended to be measured and reflected upon when assessing capital and liquidity adequacy, as well as when conducting stress testing (BIS, 2022, p. 4). As part of the risk management process, banks are strongly endorsed to assess all relevant climate risks of material nature in accordance with their risk appetite and risk frameworks in place (BIS, 2022, p. 5). The effective and efficient internal reporting to support top-level decisions regarding climate risks is reflected by Principle 7 (BIS, 2022, p. 5). The following 4 Principles stress the significance of climate risks evaluation as part of the credit, market, liquidity, and operational risks assessments (BIS, 2022, pp. 6–7). Not only that climate risks should be evaluated within individual risk assessments, but they as well have to be considered across various scenarios when assessing banks' resilience in accordance with Principle 12 (BIS, 2022, p. 7). Finally, concerning the principles pitched to supervisory bodies, BIS (2022, pp. 8–11) calls for an extensive assessment of banks' climate risk-related initiatives implemented as per Principles 1–12, as well as for the determination of an adequate reporting frequency, where supervisors are nonetheless responsible to building and ensuring the effectiveness of their own tools and techniques, as well as of their knowledge and expertise to tackle the topic at hand. While those principles call for practitioners' consideration of climate risks across all three dimensions in accordance with the Basel Framework pillars – i.e. reporting, risk management and capital adequacy – those principles are merely recommendations which lack a binding character. Nevertheless, they are narrowed to the environmental dimension of ESG, failing to address risks that might arise due to social and governance factors.

TABLE 1 BIS principles to address climate risks

Addressed to	Principle No.	Preposition
Banks	Principle 1	Banks should develop and implement a sound process for understanding and assessing the potential impacts of climate-related risk drivers on their businesses and on the environments in which they operate. Banks should consider material climate-related financial risks that could materialise over various time horizons and incorporate these risks into their overall business strategies and risk management frameworks.
	Principle 2	The board and senior management should clearly assign climate-related responsibilities to members and/or committees and exercise effective oversight of climate-related financial risks. Further, the board and senior management should identify responsibilities for climate-related risk management throughout the organisational structure.
	Principle 3	Banks should adopt appropriate policies, procedures and controls that are implemented across the entire organisation to ensure effective management of climate-related financial risks.
	Principle 4	Banks should incorporate climate-related financial risks into their internal control frameworks across the three lines of defence to ensure sound, comprehensive and effective identification, measurement and mitigation of material climate-related financial risks.
	Principle 5	Banks should identify and quantify climate-related financial risks and incorporate those assessed as material over relevant time horizons into their internal capital and liquidity adequacy assessment processes, including their stress testing programmes where appropriate.
	Principle 6	Banks should identify, monitor and manage all climate-related financial risks that could materially impair their financial condition, including their capital resources and liquidity positions. Banks should ensure that their risk appetite and risk management frameworks consider all material climate-related financial risks to which they are exposed and establish a reliable approach to identifying, measuring, monitoring and managing those risks.

TABLE 1 BIS principles to address climate risks (*cont.*)

Addressed to	Principle No.	Preposition
	Principle 7	Risk data aggregation capabilities and internal risk reporting practices should account for climate-related financial risks. Banks should seek to ensure that their internal reporting systems are capable of monitoring material climate-related financial risks and producing timely information to ensure effective board and senior management decision-making.
	Principle 8	Banks should understand the impact of climate-related risk drivers on their credit risk profiles and ensure that credit risk management systems and processes consider material climate-related financial risks.
	Principle 9	Banks should understand the impact of climate-related risk drivers on their market risk positions and ensure that market risk management systems and processes consider material climate-related financial risks.
	Principle 10	Banks should understand the impact of climate-related risk drivers on their liquidity risk profiles and ensure that liquidity risk management systems and processes consider material climate-related financial risks.
	Principle 11	Banks should understand the impact of climate-related risk drivers on their operational risk and ensure that risk management systems and processes consider material climate-related risk. Banks should also understand the impact of climate-related risk drivers on other risks and put in place adequate measures to account for these risks where material. This includes climate-related risk drivers that might lead to increasing strategic, reputational, and regulatory compliance risk, as well as liability costs associated with climate-sensitive investments and businesses.
	Principle 12	Where appropriate, banks should make use of scenario analysis to assess the resilience of their business models and strategies to a range of plausible climate-related pathways and determine the impact of climate-related risk drivers on their overall risk profile. These analyses should consider physical and transition risks as drivers of credit, market, operational and liquidity risks over a range of relevant time horizons.

TABLE 1 BIS principles to address climate risks (*cont.*)

Addressed to	Principle No.	Preposition
Supervisory bodies	Principle 13	Supervisors should determine that banks' incorporation of material climate-related financial risks into their business strategies, corporate governance and internal control frameworks is sound and comprehensive.
	Principle 14	Supervisors should determine that banks can adequately identify, monitor and manage all material climate-related financial risks as part of their assessments of banks' risk appetite and risk management frameworks.
	Principle 15	Supervisors should determine the extent to which banks regularly identify and assess the impact of climate-related risk drivers on their risk profile and ensure that material climate-related financial risks are adequately considered in their management of credit, market, liquidity, operational, and other types of risk. Supervisors should determine that, where appropriate, banks apply climate scenario analysis.
	Principle 16	In conducting supervisory assessments banks' management of climate-related financial risks, supervisors should utilise an appropriate range of techniques and tools and adopt adequate follow-up measures in case of material misalignment with supervisory expectations.
	Principle 17	Supervisors should ensure that they have adequate resources and capacity to effectively assess banks' management of climate-related financial risks.
	Principle 18	Supervisors should consider using climate-related risk scenario analysis to identify relevant risk factors, size portfolio exposures, identify data gaps and inform the adequacy of risk management approches. Supervisors may also consider the use of climate-related stress testing to evaluate a firm's financial position under severe but plausible scenarios.

Note. The table above lists the issued Principles by BIS addressing the topic of climate risk management and supervision from June 15th, 2022. (BIS, 2022, p. 2–11).

On a European level, the systemically important nature of ESG risks gained regulatory and supervisory attention as well, determining various regulatory bodies such as EBA to undergo early initiatives in addressing the prevailing ESG risks and supporting the EC's ambition of making Europe the first carbon-neutral continent over the course of the upcoming three decades. To be more specific, in December 2019, EBA issued its action plan on facilitating the transition to a green economy, committing itself to support the cash flow allocation to sustainable projects/initiatives in addition to adjusting its regulation, altering CRR II and CRD V, as well as developing new regulations and directives for investment firms (EBA, 2019, p. 6). Figure 9 below depicts EBA's mandate in accordance with the previously mentioned action plan. Concerning the banking industry, the alterations in current capital requirements directive and regulation respectively require EBA firstly to uniformly define and assess the impact of ESG risks across various timeframes, and secondly to develop mechanisms and processes through which ESG risks should be dealt with as part of financial institutions' strategic planning process and their management of risks procedures, establishing evaluation instruments to estimate the extent at

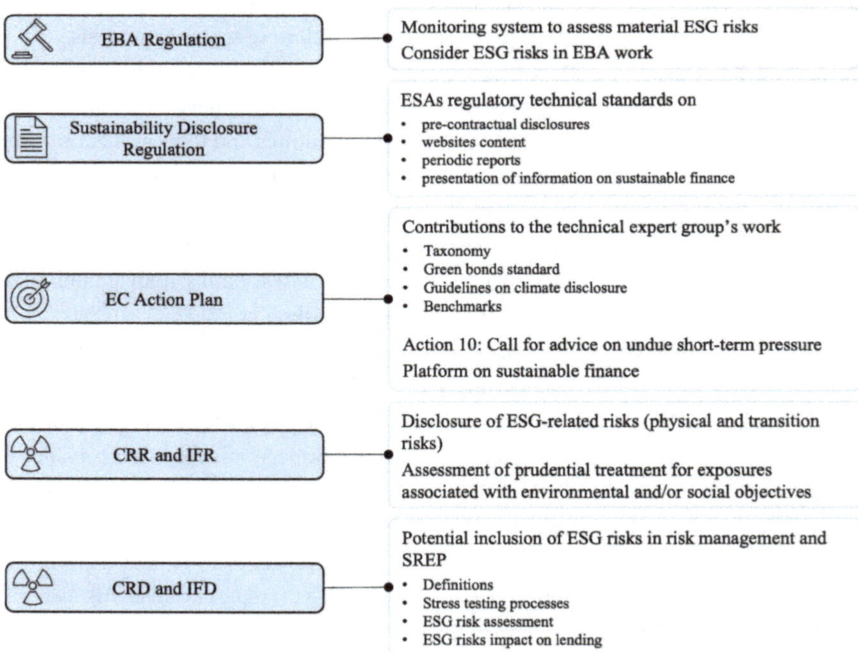

FIGURE 9 EBA deliverables for facilitating the green transition.
EBA's mandate on sustainable finance as part of its Action Plan published in December 2019 rests on five pillars as per the exhibit above.
EBA, 2019, P. 9

which ESG risks might impact banks' intermediation process (EBA, 2019, p. 6). Furthermore, in accordance with Pillar III and Pillar I, EBA's mandate rests on fostering harmonized disclosure of ESG risks across financial institutions by providing a technical standard on disclosure, and on assessing whether ESG risks necessitate additional prudential capital to ensure the system's financial stability at regional level (EBA, 2019, p. 7).

To date, the European regulatory frameworks addressing sustainability, and more precisely climate-related risks, are disclosure driven with the aim of developing a harmonized definition and understanding of ESG risks, and a classification system to facilitate decision-making. Figure 10 below depicts on a timeline key sustainability-related European regulatory initiatives conducted until June 2022, as well as prospective ones given the information available at the time this research was conducted. However, as stressed by the World Economic Forum and Wyman (2021, p. 14), the current regulatory environment for sustainability triggers a rather high degree of regulatory uncertainty due to the frequency with which sustainability regulatory frameworks adjust.

The EU Taxonomy Regulation – *Regulation (EU) 2020/825 of the European Parliament and of the Council of 18 June 2020 on the establishment of the framework to facilitate sustainable investments, and amending Regulation (EU) 2019/2088* – can be considered the first classification system implemented at the supranational level for the identification of activities which support the transition to a green economy and deliver on the agenda established within the European Green Deal (EC, 2020c, n.p.). More specifically, Article 9 states the environmental objectives of activities that are to be considered Taxonomy compliant as follows: any activity which supports the climate change mitigation and adaptation, delivers on the principles of a circular economy, prevents and controls pollution, mitigates the water waste and protects marine resources and/or protects or restore the surrounding biodiversity (European Parliament, and the

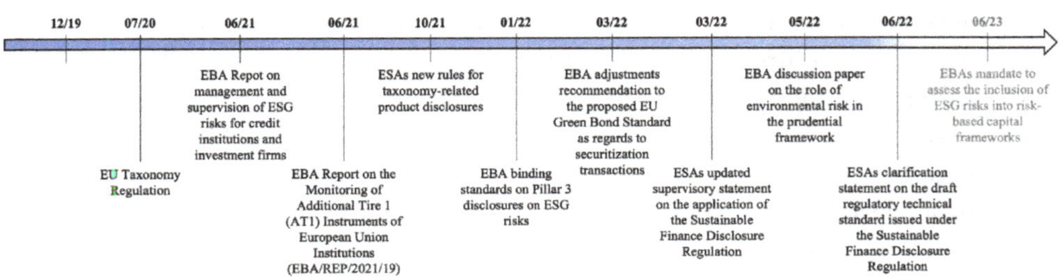

FIGURE 10 European key sustainability-related regulatory initiatives.
The exhibit above depicts on a timeline format key European regulatory initiatives addressing sustainability, where a clear focus on sustainability disclosure can be perceived.
EBA, 2022D, N.P.

Council, 2020, p. 17). In addition, delegated acts have been developed addressing the identification of activities that deliver on the first two environmental objectives, i.e. climate change mitigation and adaptation respectively, as well as the applicable methodology for both financial and non-financial institutions in disclosing information on climate-related activities, services and products entered into force January and February 2022. Therefore, the merits of the EU Taxonomy as a first classification framework for sustainability-related activities are undeniable. As identified by Lucarelli, Mazzoli, Rancan, and Severini (2020, p. 6476), there is an inverse relationship between the number of Taxonomy-derived academic studies and CO_2 emissions, i.e. reductions in the carbon dioxide levels have been reported particularly in emerging economies as the number of studies based on the EU Taxonomy evolved, determining thus the authors to acknowledge the effectiveness of the regulatory framework at hand and of associated studies in developing a common understanding of sustainable activities and in incentivizing cross-industry participation. Additionally, Schütze, Stede, Blauert, and Erdmann (2020, p. 492) acknowledged the important role of the EU Taxonomy in addressing greenwashing activities due to the increased transparency promoted by its classification system.

While the merits of the EU Taxonomy are undeniable, several limitations have been identified in the literature which should become part of the upcoming regulatory agenda to facilitate the implementation of this framework in practice. Namely, Alessi, Battiston, and Melo (2021, n.p.) assert that the current version of the Taxonomy established rather stringent criteria for activities to be considered as significantly contributing to a green economy, resulting in only a very constrained number of activities classified as eligible. Additionally, the authors emphasize that an activity is taxonomy aligned if it already transited to a sustainable alternative and does not currently undergo the transition process. Similarly, the research conducted by Schütze and Stede (2020, p. 15) stresses that activities under transition, despite significantly contributing to accumulations of GHG emissions such as building renovations, are not provided with a clear future-oriented direction that can incentivize the development of carbon-neutral innovations in the respective areas. Furthermore, while 80% of GHG emissions can be reduced by adhering to the methodology of activities classification proposed by the Taxonomy, only 20% of the labor is covered by in-scope activities, implying a wrongful assumption that labor-intensive activities can be associated with carbon-intensive ones (Schütze & Stede, 2020, p. 15). It is criticized as well that since the EU Taxonomy makes no distinction between the current activities and future projects, little incentive occurs in the long run to pursue the carbon-neutral transformation (Schütze & Stede, 2020, p. 16). The limited data availability and its questionable quality when available nonetheless trigger additional costs and resources for financial institutions when assessing the Taxonomy-compliant nature of prospective projects to be financed, leading to poorly performed risk assessments and the materialization of greenwashing (Och, 2020, p. 12).

Concerning the disclosure requirements, the European Supervisory Authorities (ESAS) recommended amendments to the *Sustainable Finance Disclosure Regulation* (SFDR), which is to be enacted as of January 1st, 2023, and is primarily focused on the periodicity of impact assessment for Taxonomy-compliant financial products, highlighting the need for the issuing institution to assess both on a pre-contractual basis and on a regular basis the environmental objective the product contributes towards in accordance with the Taxonomy Regulation (EBA, 2021c, n.p.). A series of other clarifications followed in June 2022, addressing disclosure requirements for certain financial products that include options, for the proper utilization of the developed sustainability indicators, for the disclosure of direct and indirect investments, as well as for disclosures of Taxonomy-related products (EBA, 2022c, n.p.). Yet, Och (2020, p. 11) identified a deficit in data availability for this soon-to-be-enacted regulatory framework stating that, under the current proposal, data will be available only for large corporates subject to the *Non-Financial Reporting Directive* (NFRD), where financial institutions would be deemed to rely on internally produced or outsourced proxy figures when assessing the ESG risks exposure for products to be offered to micro, as well as to small and medium-sized enterprises (SMES) for which sustainability-related disclosure is not a mandatory requirement. Additionally, as well interlinked to the EU Taxonomy are the Pillar III binding disclosure requirements published by EBA in January 2022 which include a series of climate-related ratios such as the green asset ratio (GAR) – a ratio that measures the volume of sustainability-related products offered by financial institutions in compliance with the Taxonomy – in order to facilitate investors' decision-making process regarding financial institutions (EBA, 2022b, n.p.).

Not only measures for the classification and disclosure of sustainable-related activities have been developed, but, in addition, ESG risks were defined, and recommendations to address them were made. EBA issued its *Report on Management and Supervision of ESG Risks for Credit Institutions and Investment Firms* in June 2021 where it defines ESG risks (details provided in the following section dedicated to the topic) and proposes a comprehensive implementation of initiatives addressing this category of risks on a cross-divisional basis (EBA, 2021b, pp. 10–11). Specifically, banks' strategy should be amended to consider ESG factors on a qualitative basis at a minimum over a long-time horizon that covers a 10-year timeframe and over various resilience scenarios (EBA, 2021b, pp. 10–11). Additionally, related key performance indicators (KPIs) are to be designed and disclosed accordingly, with a distinct consideration being offered to the risk-taking capacity of the respective bank (EBA, 2021b, p. 11). ESG risks into strategic frameworks should similarly be echoed when developing partnerships and when adhering to various global sustainability-driven associations, as well as when designing new or amending existing products and services offered to clients (EBA, 2021b, p. 11). Setting the tone at the top and having banks' top-level management engaged in ensuring legitimacy and the effective delivery of ESG commitments by various business units and departments, as well as establishing a dedicated sustainability committee are governance-related suggestions made by EBA (2021b, p. 11) in addition to amending top-management remuneration packages to have a long-term perspective and to include ESG driven KPIs. Lastly, in terms of risk-management frameworks, EBA (2021b, p. 11) proposes the inclusion of ESG risks into banks' assessment of their clients, where ESG risks are to be perceived as a trigger for financial risks. Likewise, banks are encouraged to identify and address data gaps, and to consider ESG risks when testing their soundness over various scenarios, developing, and incorporating nonetheless exposure matrices to be monitored on a continuous basis (EBA, 2021b, p. 11). Therefore, several similarities can be drawn with the first 12 Principles issued by the Basel Committee in June 2022. However, one could acknowledge once more the leading position European regulatory authorities assumed in regard to sustainability due to their recommendations having been issued one year prior to the publication of the aforementioned 12 Principles.

Despite the existent recommendations circulated to financial institutions for amending their risk-management frameworks in light of ESG risks, no clear guidance has been developed by regulatory bodies up to date addressing this topic. Given the concurrent focus on classifying sustainability activities, products, and services, as well as on disclosing related data nonetheless addressing ESG risks by means of increased transparency, fostering an effective and informed decision-making process as mentioned in the paragraphs above, a recalibration of this work had to occur. Arguably, varying strategic options available to institutions imply different risk exposures and ultimately determine risk-management strategies and frameworks to be implemented and adhered to (Ben-Amar et al., 2014, p. 16). Consequently, while initially intended to address ESG risk-management regulatory frameworks and procedures undertaken subsequently by industry practitioners, the existent progress in the regulatory environment determined a focus shift towards considering ESG regulatory frameworks in their entirety from a broader strategic viewpoint, assessing what are the perceived strategic implications of ESG regulatory frameworks on banks' operations.

Furthermore, the emphasis placed on disclosure requirements led to only minimal attention being allotted to changes in capital requirements as an incentive mechanism for banks to accelerate the transition to a green economy. A discussion paper was issued by EBA in May 2022 initiating the assessment of the potential inclusion of ESG risks into prudential capital requirements and setting up the preliminary framework which is to be evaluated by the industry (EBA, 2022a, n.p.). Nevertheless, based on its assessment, a recommendation will be provided to BIS by June 2023 supporting thus Basel III Finalization in regard to amending capital requirements under Pillar I for climate-related risk (EBA, 2022a, n.p.). However, contradictory opinions arose among academia who questioned the efficiency of such prudential capital reserves to address ESG risks. On the one hand, in an earlier paper, Campiglio (2016, pp. 228–229) recognizes that carbon pricing might not be sufficient enough to deliver on climate change mitigation targets and little incentive exists for banks to finance sustainability-driven projects, proposing the inclusion of green factors into banks' capital requirements and adhering to less stringent lending terms for borrowers in need of funds for transiting to less carbon-intensive operations. By contrast, Baker and Wurgler (2015, p. 315) state that any increase in capital requirements will lead ultimately to higher costs of capital. Similarly, Gursoy (2016, p. 72) argues that stringent capital requirements will negatively affect banks' incentives to engage in green financing unless a distinction is made between green and brown investments, with less capital being required for the former investment type. Likewise, due to their nature of resulting in financial risks already covered within the existent capital requirements, a question might arise if ESG risks should be perceived as an additional risk category or, contrastingly, a risk driver in which case little or no amendments to capital requirements would be necessary. Similarly, Zetzsche and Anker-Sørensen (2022, p. 47) advocate against the amendment of capital requirements pre-maturely given the current level of addressing ESG considerations in the regulatory environment, recommending amending risk-management frameworks and top-management remuneration packages as means of incentivizing green financing.

Further limitations of the current regulatory frameworks and initiatives addressing sustainability were emphasized in the available literature. Ahlström (2019, p. 450) criticizes the current voluntary nature of regulatory frameworks which do not incentivize enough market participants to engage in sustainability-related activities. Furthermore, he emphasizes the absence of sustainability concepts from the existing EU company law, attributing it to a compartmentalizing phenomenon where each sector addresses sustainability differently, leading to an uncoordinated view on the topic (Ahlström, 2019, p. 450). Additionally, Zetzsche and Anker-Sørensen (2022, pp. 64–71) list as further market challenges faced by industry practitioners when adhering to changes in the regulatory environment the lack of expertise and expert consensus, of data that establishes a correlation and causation link between ESG-driven initiatives and the field of finance, as well as the inconsistent application of regulatory frameworks given the diverse implementation timeframes established at a national level. Subsequently, as a reaction to a frequently adjusting regulatory environment tackling the topic of sustainability, banks were determined to amend their business models and strategic directions. Thus regulation can be considered one of the key drivers of change in the banking landscape. The second key driver for change consists of the ESG risks themselves faced by financial institutions in their operations. Therefore, the following two sections will provide details on the definition of ESG risks and their systemically important nature, as well as on the changing banking environment to address existent regulatory stimuli.

5 Environmental, Social and Governance (ESG) Risks

While the benefits of sustainability are well-known and universally quoted, its challenges cannot be overlooked. One major challenge experienced by credit institutions when engaging in sustainability-related activities consists of ESG risks, representing the third element of the conceptual framework developed to guide the study at hand. EBA (2021b, p. 33) defines ESG risks as any potential financial negative impact of ESG factors on a credit institution, arising either from the activities conducted by the institution itself, i.e. from the invested assets, or by its customers. Therefore, an "outside-in" and an "inside-out" perspective hold, where the former consists of both changes in the surrounding environment that can affect the physical locations of financial institutions, or of client-performed activities with an impact on banks' core businesses, while the latter is primarily concerned with institutions' own contributions to ESG factors such as via their GHG emissions (EBA, 2021b, pp. 29–30). These risks, regardless of whether they are classified as physical or transition risks, will undergo a transformation process, resulting ultimately in financial risks that can potentially negatively impact the financial system's stability, as depicted in Figure 11 below (EBA, 2021b, p. 34). Comparably, Carè (2018c, p. 49) recognizes the direct, as well as the indirect contributions of banks to addressing ESG risks via implementing sustainability initiatives on a business-as-usual basis, or by respectively offering green products and services to their clients.

Beginning with the environmental risks, a distinction can be made between physical risks, i.e. risks arising from changes in climatological aspects, as well

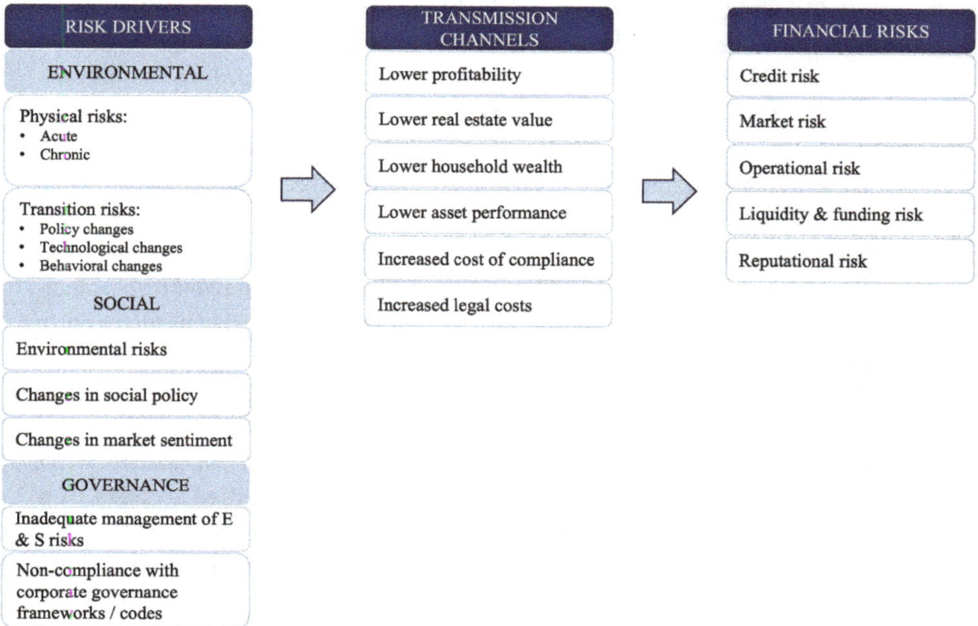

FIGURE 11 ESG risk drivers, their transmission channels, and subsequent market impact. The figure above depicts ESG risks for all three pillars, their transmission channels, as well as how they will ultimately materialize in financial risks.
EBA, 2021B, P. 34

as transition risks related to transformations in the core business of financial institutions themselves or of their counterparts (EBA, 2021b, pp. 34–41). While acute physical risks represent negative financial effects on the performance of financial institutions arising from a particular climate shock experienced by either the banks' customers or by the institution via its' invested assets, including floods, fires, or drought, chronic physical risks occur progressively over a longer period of time and consist of, for example, a progressive rise in the sea level or temperature, as well as losses in the biodiversity or land productivity (EBA, 2021b, p. 34). Such physical risks are deemed to affect the economy in its entirety. On the supply side, extreme climate events have an impact on both human health and on institutions' plant and equipment, yielding distressed labor and a decrease in the useful life of paraphernalia used in operations, determining companies to relocate their investments to sustaining operations instead of increasing efficiency, as well as increased price volatility for food items (Breitenfellner, Pointner, & Schuberth, 2019, p. 58). On the demand side, increased cautionary savings to withstand climate shocks decrease the disposable income and the level of consumption (Breitenfellner et al., 2019,

p. 59). Similarly, NGFS (2021, p. 10) highlights the negative economic consequences of acute physical risks due to the underlying disturbances of certain business-performed activities and property damages. Regarding the chronic physical risks, due to their gradual nature of occurring, a need for high capital investments and effort to contain and, in the best case, reverse the trend is acknowledged, calling for involvement from various market participants including authorities and regulatory bodies, corporates, as well as societies on a broader level (NGFS, 2021, p. 10).

Transition risks, on the other hand, are predominantly derived from uncertainties surrounding the timing and complexities faced by market participants in transitioning to green and sustainable economies, be them driven by changes in the regulatory environment, technological changes, and/or by changes in customers' and investors' behavior who exert pressure on companies and financial institutions to accelerate the green transformation (EBA, 2021b, p. 41). According to NGFS (2021, p. 10), transition risks are deemed to negatively impact financial institutions due to the transition costs borne by companies and households, which subsequently reduce the latter's profitability and wealth respectively, and impede their ability to deliver on their credit obligations. By contrast, regulatory initiatives incentivizing banks to accelerate their contributions to the green transition via their lending mechanism can make funding less accessible for certain industries such as aviation where technological changes to reduce GHG emissions are harder to develop and implement (Breitenfellner et al., 2019, p. 59).

More importantly, physical and transition risks should not be assessed on an individual basis given that they are interrelated. To be more specific, negative climatological factors, as well as unsustainable activities performed by market participants are the triggers of, for example, regulatory amendments that might pose subsequently transition risks to corporates and institutions subject to those changes (EBA, 2021b, p. 42). By contrast, while transition measures can significantly reduce physical risks, the lengthier the time needed for companies to deliver on the green transformation, the more severe those physical risks will become (EBA, 2021b, p. 42). Therefore, when it comes to regulatory reforms, following the principles of parsimony, less complex solutions might be somewhat more efficient. However, as mentioned in the previous section, the current European regulatory landscape addressing sustainability tends to be characterized by complex frameworks which adapt frequently, triggering thus not only regulatory uncertainty but also leading to a potential increase in the severity of physical risks.

Currently, as highlighted in the section above as well, the focus lies primarily on environmental risks. Yet, social and governance risks cannot be overlooked, given their nature deemed to result, similar to environmental risks, in financial risks. Therefore, EBA (2021b, pp. 43–47) defines social risks as any current, or perspective, negative financial impact on market participants' solvency and/or performance due to adverse social factors which include, but are not limited to, inequality, health, safety, and security, or changes in human capital. Likewise, governance risks can have alike impacts on the financial system and the economy as environmental or social risks have, however, they stream from factors such as corruption, bribery, management remuneration packages, board independence, internal controls, or the degree to which environmental and social considerations are implemented at higher organizational levels and their legitimacy acknowledged and facilitated by top management personnel (EBA, 2021b, pp. 47–49). Therefore, when implementing initiatives to address environmental concerns, it is highly important for market participants to consider nonetheless the impacts such initiatives can have on social and governance factors. When addressing thus the S and G pillars concurrent to the E pillar, the topic complexity is considerably increased indicating towards another trade-off as mentioned in the paragraph above which cannot be disregarded.

As previously defined, ESG risks undergo a transformation process, resulting in financial systemically important risks. A parallel has been made between climatological extreme events such as droughts, hurricanes, or earthquakes and financial distress where the former negatively impacted for example sustainable harvesting, and the subsequent economic well-being of farmers who were unable to satisfy their financing commitments triggering bank losses (University of Cambridge Institute for Sustainability Leadership, 2014, p. 11). Breitenfellner et al. (2019, p. 60) emphasize the existence of a liability risk in which case claims for negative impacts on one's operations due to GHG emissions produced by someone else cannot be internalized given the widespread nature of the pollution phenomenon across legislations. This liability risk contributes to financial distress via two channels: firstly, the increased number of insurance claims might not be adequately addressed in the risk calculation models of insurance companies whose distress might cascade to various financial market participants given their interconnectedness; secondly, investors' assessment of assets can be biased in the absence of adequate data and impact the effectiveness with which sustainability-related activities conducted by companies are assessed (Breitenfellner et al., 2019, p. 60).

However, it was identified that ESG initiatives conducted by financial institutions can address and moderate the systemic effect of such risks as the ones mentioned throughout this section. Aevoae, Andrieș, Ongena, and Sprincean (2022, p. 8), conducting a study on the impact of sustainability ratings of 365 publicly traded banks of both large and small sizes across 47 countries on the systemic risk, acknowledged that a negative correlation exists between the dependent variable, i.e. the systemic risk, and the independent variable, i.e. ESG score. Similarly, the authors assessed that while ESG activities, particularly those targeted toward the governance pillar, can reduce the risk of systemic market failure, those activities can nonetheless decrease the exposure of banks to failure during times of market distress (Aevoae et al., 2022, p. 10).

Due to their systemically important nature that can negatively impact the well-functioning of the financial system and of the overall economy, ESG risks have to be operationalized across business units. Consequently, EBA (2021b, pp. 10–11) recommends that ESG risks should be addressed by financial institutions across various dimensions, being therefore incorporated into banks' business strategy, governance, and risk management practices respectively as stated in the previous section. Therefore, with authorities stressing the need of integrating ESG risks into various operations conducted by financial institutions, the banking industry was deemed to experience changes. Consequently, the following section will detail the identified amendments occurring in the banking sector to address these current sustainability-related challenges.

6 An Adjusting Banking Industry

New regulatory requirements as a reaction to ESG risks, as well as the ESG risks themselves, initiated adjustments in strategies employed by banks when conducting their business. As opposed to the regular transformation of deposits into loans, mortgages, and financing instruments for retail and corporate clients, further attention has to be granted to environmental, social, and governance aspects. Given the broad applicability of the topic not only externally across industries, but also internally across divisions and business units, banks tend to amend their strategies to account for sustainability, aiming at positioning themselves in sync or, when possible, ahead of the market. In addition to adjusting their products and services, banks also amended their internal operations and governance structures, all to address contemporary ESG market realities. Therefore, the fourth element of the developed conceptual framework focuses on changes occurring in the banking system that reflect sustainability considerations prevailing in the industry.

To address current challenges streaming from environmental and social issues confronted by societies globally, the field of social and sustainable finance emerged. Carè (2018b, p. 16) acknowledges the transition to "*financial humanism*" in the aftermath of the 2007–2008 financial crisis, where the financial system encountered a transformation characterized by a focus shift towards climate and social-related aspects, as opposed to profitability only. As a consequence, despite being coined differently as sustainable, green, ethical, alternative, or value-based banks, credit institutions engage in providing financing in manners that can support external stakeholders, i.e. the society and the environment, in transitioning to a sustainable and prosperous future (Carè, 2018b, p. 17). Similarly, Igbudu, Garanti, and Popoola (2018, pp. 4050–4051) define a sustainable business model as one oriented towards enhancing and preserving societies' well-being, by providing products and services consistent with environmental and social conditions.

Several strategic directions can be identified across banks which incorporate the concepts characterizing sustainability. While relatively similar in structures, banks' strategies addressing sustainability differ content-wise, as well as in terms of the driving motives, be them environmental, social, or business-related motives (Zimmermann, 2019, p. 2268). However, there are several characteristics that distinguish traditional commercial banks from their environmentally friendly and socially responsible counterparts. Lalon (2015, p. 35) enunciates the following characteristics of banks which give them a green status: banks utilize automation and online banking as supporting tools for sustainable development; safety and security of customers and societies as a whole, as well as green investments are prioritized; ESG considerations strived for outside the banks are mirrored within the organization; cost reductions and energy savings are considered as contributing to an increased local gross domestic product; banks provide advisory and knowledge to stakeholders, engaging thus in literacy programs and raising awareness at a larger scale. Additionally, as part of sustainable banking, the socially responsible investment (SRI) is considered an ideological foundation, which, particularly in the banking industry, focuses on banks' initiatives of providing cheaper funding for sustainable and socially responsible projects, while penalizing brown, high emission producing and socially undesirable projects with stricter lending terms and higher interest rates (Idbudu et al., 2018, p. 4051).

When implementing a sustainability-related strategy, banks can approach the topic from different perspectives. Specifically, Zimmermann (2019, pp. 2274–2276), by conducting a case study on 26 German banks, acknowledged the presence of five different types of strategies addressing ESG considerations. Firstly, the author highlights the narrow strategy where sustainability considerations are limited to green products which are however not adequately advertised to clients, and where financial institutions engage in sponsoring without clear social-based screening criteria. Additionally, sustainability is not implemented as part of the bank's core business due to a perceived lack of economic benefits, and no specific organizational function is allocated to ESG (Zimmermann,

2019, p. 2274). Banks operating a peripheral strategy differentiate themselves from the previous ones in that they developed investment products for social and environmental projects, where funds are allocated based on certain well-established criteria (Zimmermann, 2019, p. 2275). Furthermore, attention is allocated by those banks to the sustainable nature of in-house operations, having developed measures to address for example energy efficiency issues, aspects of business trips, as well as employees' health and work-life balance management. The balanced strategy, while still driven by business rationales including profit generation or risk reduction when sustainability initiatives are considered, can be characterized by having developed various green and social products, as well as engaging in university-led partnerships for research and future development purposes (Zimmermann, 2019, p. 2275). The last two business strategies which implement sustainability in the core business and are driven by social and environmental motives in addition to the economic ones only are the integrated strategies with a focus on social or environmental aspects respectively (Zimmermann, 2019, p. 2276). Therefore, banks' sustainability efforts can be determined based on the extent to which ESG considerations are adopted in their processes and products/services offered to clients.

According to Carè (2018a, pp. 65–66), credit institutions assume a triple role in supporting sustainability, as follows: firstly, through their function of redirecting the capital flow, they can develop green products for their clients and engage in advisory services as means of client literacy; secondly, banks can percept environmental stimuli as they occur and provide regulatory bodies with feedback on how policies can be amended to reflect contemporary conditions; lastly, via communication, their reputation can be enhanced, delivering on the green requirements of various external stakeholders such as investors or the society the bank serves. This highlights one more time the noteworthy role credit institutions have in helping the economy to effectively transition by means of capital allocation to green projects, by raising awareness among and educating their clients, as well as by supporting the development of regulatory suitable topic-related frameworks that establish a level-playing filed for all market participants.

Addressing the first identified role of banks in supporting the transition to a green economy, while various green products and services exist to satisfy customers' preferences and a growing demand for sustainability, Carè (2018a, pp. 69–74) emphasizes the following products as the most prevailing ones: home mortgages and commercial building loans characterized by below-market interest rates and thus affordable for a broader client spectrum, as well as by ensuring energy efficiency; green credit cards which provide donations for purchases conducted by the card's owner; microfinance, particularly supported at the EU level, though which small and medium-sized businesses are provided the capital that they would otherwise not receive by means of credit for supporting sustainability projects; green bonds which are designed in their entirety to support the sustainable transformation by making capital available to environmental projects, as well as associated funds and indices. Other less frequently quoted instruments are impact investment funds, green fiscal funds, and debt-for-nature swaps (Carè, 2018a, p. 74).

Sustainability considerations occur not only at the product and service level. Conducting a study on sixteen banks operating in Europe, Nosratabadi et al. (2020, p. 2328) identified that environmental and social aspects are as well implemented into banks' value proposition, their financial aspects when considering the customers to be served, as well as when engaging in partnerships and becoming members of sustainability-related associations. Likewise, Carè (2018a, p. 66) stresses that banks committed to sustainability engage in active communication with their stakeholders, highlighting thus the key role of performing non-financial disclosure. On the topic of external communication, Lalon (2015, p. 37) as well details the green marketing initiatives conducted by banks achieved by means of first, product characteristics adjustments, complemented by related advertising campaigns. Additionally, banks implement various measures addressing sustainability as part of their operations and the operations of offices/branches. Credit institutions tackle sustainability not only through measuring and improving their energy consumption via energy efficiency initiatives such as the utilization of solar panels to electrify their offices but also by implementing measures to address water and paper waste (Lalon, 2015, p. 36). Consequently, it can be stated that credit institutions engaging in ESG consider both the inside-out and the outside-in perspectives applicable to ESG factors, taking internal measures to deliver on, for example, climate goals, as opposed to supporting their clients' transition only.

Nevertheless, amendments occurred regarding the governance aspects of credit institutions. Specifically, a shift arose from the "*shareholder theory*" which advocates for strategies maximizing shareholders' returns only, to the "*stakeholder theory*" which supports the implementation of strategies serving the interest of a broader category of stakeholders, including the general public (Miralles-Quirós et al., 2019, p. 1405). Focusing particularly on the Board structure and its female representation, Birindelli et al. (2018, pp. 4710–4711) conducted a study on 108 banks operating both in the US and Europe and asserted that, once the female headcount in the Board reaches its optimum level, i.e. approximately a third of the Board representation, the marginal effect of increasing the female representation on bank's performance is minimal, marking thus the concave nature between Board diversification and ESG performance. While the authors recognized that a balance between the number of male and female Board members tends to be positively correlated with the performance of a credit institution as driven by an increase in the efficiency and effectiveness of communication and problem-solving capability, they cannot fully confirm the "*dual critical mass*" theory, as firstly formulated by Schwartz-Ziv (2017, p. 754) with their identified concave relationship. According to Schwartz-Ziv (2017, p. 778), Boards whose composition consists of an equal number of male and female members, i.e. three members representatives for each gender, will be more efficient and active in decision-making. Furthermore, Birindelli et al. (2018, p. 4711) emphasize that not only the Board's gender diversity can positively impact the ESG performance and ultimately trigger a higher ESG score for the respective bank, but also its size and the existence of a committee addressing corporate social responsibility matters. By contrast, the independence of Board members inversely correlates with banks' sustainability-related performance (Birindelli et al., 2018, p. 4711).

Several ESG-related initiatives have been identified by academia as being performed by banks to address the current regulatory environment and sustainability-related challenges. Be them green products or financial instruments for ESG projects, sustainability-related employees and client literacy programs, or amendments in the internal operational processes and governance structures, banks shifted their focus from generating shareholders' profitability only, to considering the interest of a broader group of stakeholders, including, but not being limited to, the societies in which banks operate and the surrounding environment. However, Nosratabadi et al. (2020, p. 2328) stress the challenging nature of establishing and employing a sustainable business model which can address both ESG issues and generate expected shareholders' returns. Therefore, in the absence of a clearly identifiable regulatory advantage for pursuing sustainability-related initiatives, credit institutions tend to be rather reluctant toward accelerating their efforts. This can be nevertheless observed in the results yielded by EBA's exercise conducted in 2021 at the EU level which stresses a concerning regional-wide GAR of 7.9%, denoting subsequently the somewhat minimal progress achieved to date (EBA, 2021d, p. 7). Consequently, as it will be detailed in the following section, ESG initiatives performed by banks tend to have varying and sometimes contradictory effects on banks' performance as measured by either profitability or risk-appetite and risk-taking capabilities, which can nonetheless justify some of the reluctance exhibited by financial institutions to today toward giving course to ESG-driven strategic directions.

7 Sustainability Implementation – a Strategic Opportunity or Burden?

As presented in the previous section, financial institutions' strategies tended to commence modifications to reflect current regulatory amendments triggered by ESG risks and sustainability regulatory considerations. Once the latter elements became topics of interest among various market participants, as well as widely acknowledged, the number of studies conducted by academia increased who assessed and measured the degree to which ESG aspects embodied in banks' operations, products, and overall strategies affect banks' profitability and risk character. However, contradictory opinions have occurred and while one body of research acknowledged the positive contributions made by ESG-driven strategies, other academics expressed a rather reluctant attitude toward the effectiveness of such sustainability initiatives performed by banks. Consequently, the remainder of this section addresses the last element of the conceptual framework designed to guide this study and elaborates on the extent to which ESG can be associated with a strategic opportunity or, by contrast, a strategic challenge to financial institutions and their performance, based on quantitative studies conducted by academic researchers.

Beginning with banks' profitability as an internal financial measure of performance, mixed results were identified in the existing literature on whether ESG practices and associated disclosures can positively contribute to shareholders' value creation or, by contrast, can damage it. Buallay's (2019, p. 110) research on 235 banks operating in the European Union covering the timeframe between 2007–2016, measured the impact of the ESG-related disclosure on banks' operational, financial, and market performance as determined by the return-on-assets (ROA), return-on-equity (ROE) and Tobin's Q respectively. It has been recognized that ESG disclosure in its entirety has positive impacts on all three performance measures. Yet, varied outcomes were obtained when the three pillars were considered individually, as follows: while the climate-related disclosure enhances EU banks' financial and market profitability – i.e. climate-related initiatives are taken into consideration in investors' decisions – the value-destroying nature of the corporate social responsibility (CSR) disclosure was identified for all employed measures of performance (Buallay, 2019, p. 110). Furthermore, both positive and negative results were yielded for the G pillar where its disclosure was associated with value creation only for the studied market parameter (Buallay, 2019, p. 111).

Similar results were obtained by Miralles-Quirós et al. (2019, pp. 1412–1413) whose study assessed the extent to which banks' involvement in ESG activities can be reflected in enhanced value creation to banks' shareholders. The academia support that particularly the E and G activities have the potential to drive value creation given their positive and statistically significant relationship with market performance indicators. However, a negative relationship could have been established between the social pillar and shareholders' value creation – social activities oriented towards employees, customers and the society as a whole appear to be value-destroying due to the higher costs of implementation above the subsequently derived benefits (Miralles-Quirós et al., 2019, p. 1413). Therefore, it can be stated that a strong corporate governance able to ensure transparency and accountability tends to be preferred by shareholders over employee-oriented and societal-oriented actions (Miralles-Quirós et al., 2019, p. 1417).

Bătae, Dragomir, and Feleagă (2021, pp. 14–15), conducting their research on European banks for a 10-year timeframe covering the period post-crises to 2019, confirmed the positive impact of decarbonization and waste management initiatives undertaken by banks on their ROE, ROA, as well as on their future stock market performance, validating the competitive advantage banks are deemed to achieve by means of delivering on decarbonization and waste management strategies. By contrast, banks' commitment to developing socially responsible products negatively impacts their profitability and damages shareholder value creation (Bătae et al., 2021, p. 15). Consequently, based on the above-mentioned studies, it could be derived that credit institutions can improve their performance by means of engaging in climate-related initiatives. Such improved performance due to delivering on environmental-related objectives corresponds with the current regulatory focus which predominantly addresses the E pillar of ESG. By contrast, despite being equally important, the social pillar received less attention to date from regulatory authorities and hence no regulatory competitive advantage is perceived to occur which ultimately disincentivizes banks to undergo socially focused strategic directions. Nevertheless, with a strong focus on banks' engagement in supporting the transition to a green economy, investors tend to disregard banks' contributions towards the S pillar and to attribute little if any value to such contributions, which is deemed to consequently result in negative effects on banks' performance as indicated by the aforementioned studies.

Contradicting the above-mentioned studies which deem the environmental and governance aspects as being value drivers, conducting a study on 93 banks operating in emerging markets during 2015–2018 to assess the relationship between ESG considerations and banks' performance as measured by ROA and ROE, Shakil, Mahmood, Tasnia, and Munim (2019, pp. 1337–1339) acknowledged the positive impacts yielded by not only the environmental activities but also by the social initiatives on banks' ROE, at a 5% significance level. However, no statistically significant result has been identified for the ROA performance indicator (Shakil et al., 2019, p. 1339). Nevertheless, consistent with the perception of a weak governance structure that lacks governmental and regulatory support, and which characterizes developing economies, no statistically significant relationship has been identified between the G pillar of ESG and banks' financial performance (Shakil et al., 2019, p. 1339). Thus, when evaluating the relationship between ESG-driven actions undertaken by banks and the impact on their performance, it is of utmost importance that other factors are accounted for such as the development stage of the economy in the country in which the respective credit institutions conduct their business, i.e. developed or emerging.

The limited power of ESG-related strategies on banks' profitability was recognized by Azmi et al. (2021, p. 16) who acknowledged the presence of a diminishing return to scale phenomenon in emerging markets, where ESG activities can increase banks' value only when performed until a certain level at which stakeholders' indifference is reached and the curve of marginal effect marks a turning point; thus, the shareholder theory is only partially empirically supported by the study at hand. Results of comparable nature were identified by El Khoury, Nasrallah, and Alareeni (2021, p. 15) when investigating the relationship between ESG frameworks and banks' performance in the MENAT region – i.e. Middle East, North Africa and Turkey. Precisely, the researchers support that sustainability responsible initiatives conducted at the banks level improve banks' financial performance up until a certain threshold is touched which once exceeded, the costs start overweighting the benefits and thus ESG activities turn into value-destroying ones, indicating a concave relationship between the two variables. By contrast, environmental-related initiatives only have a convex relationship with the market KPI, indicating that there is no incentive for banks to engage in climate-related activities as these investments will not be rewarded in the short term (El Khoury et al., 2021, p. 17).

Contradicting the positive or the limited aforementioned impacts, in a later study commenced on credit institutions operating both in developed and emerging markets, while researching the link between ESG disclosure and the performance of banks in the aftermath of the 2007–2008 financial crisis, Buallay et al. (2021, p. 764) stressed that all three measures of performance, i.e. ROA, ROE and Tobin's Q, are negatively affected by ESG disclosure regardless whether the bank is originating from a developed or, by contrast, from a developing country, contradicting nonetheless the stakeholder theory where higher profitability can be determined by sustainability- and socially-responsible activities performed by financial institutions. Likewise, Valls Martínez, Cruz

Rambaud, and Parra Oller (2020, p. 18) identified that a lack of differentiation exists between an ethical as opposed to a conventional banking business model in terms of profitability. Additionally, as discovered in an earlier paper by Baker and Wurgler (2015, p. 319), an increase in capital requirements due to sustainability will increase the cost of financing for banks, as measured by the weighted average cost of capital, reducing subsequently banks' profitability. Yet, Azmi et al. (2021, p. 16) emphasized the effect of ESG on the cost of equity only, as follows: while the cost of debt, and implicitly the default risk of banks, are not impacted by ESG performance, by contrast, banks' cost of equity is expected to decline with an increase in ESG activities, indicating a damaging effect of sustainability-related initiatives on shareholders' value creation. Those results could potentially be attributed to the current pricing mechanism which fails to differentiate between green and brown investments. Namely, up until today, no capital requirements amendments were made to reflect banks' involvement in supporting the green transition and to differentiate between market players with a green versus brown balance sheet. However, once such a distinction will materialize, early-stage movers are expected to find themselves with a competitive advantage over their peers with limited engagement in sustainability.

The second internal performance dimension considered by researchers when assessing the role of ESG-driven strategies is represented by banks' stability, as determined by their risk-taking appetite, solvency, and liquidity. However, these studies yielded as well mixed results and, one more time, contradictory opinions among academia could have been identified. Focusing on banks being incorporated and operating in Europe, Di Tommaso and Thornton (2020, pp. 2291–2295) contradict the previous studies which yielded a positive effect of ESG-driven strategies on banks' value, arguing that a tradeoff exists which cannot be overlooked, i.e. while ESG performance reduces risk-taking through banks committing their resources to sustainability linked projects considered low-risk, banks' value will be reduced in short-term given that ESG investments are only profitable in the long-run. Analogously, by comparing an ethical business model with the traditional one of commercial banks in Europe from a financial and economic standpoint, Valls Martínez et al. (2020, pp. 17–19) concluded that banks that consider the well-being of their customers, of the societies in which they operate and of the surrounding environment as opposed to profitability only that characterizes traditional banking models can achieve improved liquidity and solvency positions, making them less risky.

Toth, Lippai-Makra, Szladek, and Kis (2021, pp. 441–446), in their study of commercial banks operating in the European regions, support the positive contributions of ESG initiatives on non-performing loans. Specifically, the authors identified a negative statistically significant relationship between banks' sustainability practices and the amount of non-performing loans, indicating thus an improved risk position where capital requirements incentivize banks to engage in risk mitigation activities more truthfully. Therefore, considering these results, one could derive that capital requirements amendments via a reward or penalizing system might positively contribute not only to accelerating banks' commitment towards delivering on their sustainability-linked objectives but also improve their risk position.

By contrast, despite the ability to generate long-term sustainable returns, green investments are nevertheless expected to alter banks' resilience to ESG risks (Pyka & Nocoń, 2021, p. 3512). CSR activities tend to have a positive effect on a bank's solvency under normal market conditions only (Gutiérrez-López & Abad-González, 2020, p. 2586). Yet, when the market experiences distress conditions, the power of CSR for supporting banks' stability does not hold (Gutiérrez-López & Abad-González, 2020, p. 2586). This finding was conversely contradicted by Chiaramonte et al. (2021, pp. 1174–1175) whose research at the European level identified a positive relationship between ESG activities and banks' stability during crisis scenarios, given the increased prudential attitude of banks which triggers increased confidence among its customers and subsequently an improved reputation.

Yet, mixed results are expected to occur based on the size of banks included in the study. Therefore, a more recent paper conducted globally on 473 commercial banks assessed the relationship between banks' stability and the inclusion, as well as the performance of ESG initiatives, given different bank sizes as measured by the total assets (Albdiwy, Wan Ahmed, & Abd Sukor, 2022, p. 405). Albdiwy et al. (2022, p. 405) identified that the stability of large banks whose total assets are valued above log 14 will be positively influenced by the implementation of sustainability frameworks. By contrast, medium- and small-size banks will experience higher costs of implementation which will, in turn, negatively impact their stability. When the three sustainability pillars were considered on an individual basis, similar results were obtained for the first two elements, i.e. environmental and social aspects (Albdiwy et al., 2022, pp. 405–406). Yet, it appears that the stability of smaller and medium-sized banks tends to be positively affected by a strongly addressed governance structure as highlighted by the yielded positive statistically significant relationship at a 5% significance level (Albdiwy et al., 2022, p. 407).

While most of the studies focused on analyzing the financial impact of ESG considerations on banks' performance, some academics took a step back, assessing the non-financial effect on banks' ESG performance of various bank elements such as the gender diversity of the Board, or the implementation of

CSR considerations, which will subsequently via their impact on the ESG performance translate into financial effects. Shakil, Tasnia, and Mostafiz (2020, p. 668), conducting a study on 37 banks in the United States during a timeframe of 5 years between 2013–2017, identified that gender diversity at the Board level is positively correlated to banks' ESG performance due to the fact that female Board members are perceived as being driven by higher ethicality and possessing interpersonal skills that facilitate legitimacy of ESG practices. By contrast, Bătae et al. (2021, pp. 15–16) concluded that the G pillar has not been identified as contributing to enhanced bank profitability, contradicting the extent to which Boards' diversity can yield superior shareholder returns. Additionally, Di Tommaso and Thornton (2020, p. 2291) support that banks' governance has statistically significant impacts on the risk-taking appetite of banks, where Boards' diversity and independence are negatively correlated with risk-taking, while the opposite holds for the number of Board members.

Bank-customers relationships as measured by loyalty and trust have been identified to be improved through sustainability-related initiatives performed by banks (Ibe-enwo, Igbudu, Garanti, & Popoola, 2019, p. 11). More specifically, the survey conducted by Ibe-enwo et al. (2019, p. 10) with 551 banks' customers from North Cyprus, assessed that both customers' loyalty and their trust are positively correlated to a green image banks receive by proactively implementing ESG in their business strategies and processes. Yet, while a green bank image positively influences customers' trust and loyalty, no statistically significant relationship was determined between the latter, indicating thus that banks have to consider both building loyalty and trust via their green initiatives, as opposed to assuming that trust will be subsequently translated into clients' loyalty (Ibo-enwo et al., 2019, p. 10). Similar results have been obtained in an earlier study conducted by Igbudu et al. (2018, p. 4057) who advocate for the competitive advantage banks can achieve through enhancing clients' loyalty by means of engaging in ESG practices and developing a green corporate image, where the latter is positively correlated with stakeholders' loyalty. Emphasizing the role of reputation on the short-term returns of banks, El Khoury et al. (2021, p. 17) likewise assessed a concave relationship between the social pillar of ESG and various operational and market performance indicators.

To this end, one could agree on the complexity imposed by the topic of sustainability given its mixed empirical results on banks' internal and external performance. On the one hand, proof has been brought by academia that ESG activities performed by banks can yield a positive financial, operational, and market performance, to a certain extent, particularly if all three pillars are equally addressed. On the other hand, ESG initiatives were deemed as being profitable in the long term only, which is not compatible with the rather short-term view of investors. Nevertheless, the risk attitude of banks tends to be altered by ESG considerations, resulting one more time in contradictory opinions, i.e. while some researchers deliberate on the stability of banks as being improved by ESG activities due to an enhanced reputation, as well as by leveraging on the positive effects brought to loyalty and trust, other academics express their reluctancy, affirming that banks' stability on the basis of ESG consideration holds only under normal market conditions, and not during crises scenarios. Consequently, the remainder of this paper will summarize and discuss the findings enunciated throughout this research paper, providing an answer to the stated research questions, and ultimately concluding with a series of final remarks, limitations, and areas of future potential research.

8 Discussions

Given the novelty of the sustainability topic and the attention it received over the past years once the impacts of climate change have been acknowledged as posing an imminent threat to future generations to come, the number of studies approaching the topic from several different perspectives considerably increased. It has been nevertheless identified that an increase in the number of sustainability-related studies, and particularly an increase in those related to the EU Taxonomy framework which established a classification system for green activities, can positively impact the environment by being negatively correlated to CO_2 levels (Lucarelli et al., 2020, p. 6476). Therefore, one could derive that through conducting various studies, the level of public awareness is enhanced, and the commitment to delivering on the urgent public goal to decarbonize the planet is embraced by market players across industries. However, when it comes to the banking industry, its fundamental role in driving the transition to a green sustainable economy through its funding mechanism and its ability to redirect cash flows to sustainability-driven projects was acknowledged by the EC (2020a, n.p.), as well as by various academia. Consequently, addressing the identified knowledge gap, the study at hand aims to answer the following main research question: *What are the perceived strategic implications derived from European sustainability risk management regulatory frameworks for credit institutions?* To provide an answer to this question, four other questions had to be firstly addressed and will be detailed in the remaining of this section.

Regulation, and specifically financial regulation, can be perceived as a mechanism through which behaviors can be influenced, and thus a support factor to facilitate the transition (Ahlström, 2019, p. 450). Therefore, to derive an answer to the above-stated question, the identification of core European regulatory initiatives addressing sustainability was assessed as a pre-requisite. At the European level, focusing particularly on the banking industry, ESG risks started to be rigorously addressed once EBA (2019, p. 6) published at the end of 2019 its action plan on sustainable finance, committing itself to not only defining ESG risks but to as well develop supporting mechanisms for the identification and implementation of sustainability-driven risks in both banks' strategies and their risk-management frameworks, leading ultimately to amendments in the CRR II and CRD V. Additionally, as part of its commitments to contribute to developments in supranational banking regulatory frameworks, EBA was mandated to foster, as part of Pillar III of the Basel Framework, harmonized ESG risks disclosure across banks operating in the EU member states via a disclosure technical standard, as well as to assess the extent to which ESG risks might necessitate additional capital reserves from banks to ensure the stability of the financial system, addressing any potential systemic shocks (EBA, 2019, p. 7).

To date, the focus in the European Union is on disclosure regulation where a major milestone was achieved with the publication of the EU Taxonomy Regulation in June 2020, and of its subsequent acts which established the first classification system for activities considered green and thus positively contributing to continental decarbonization (EC, 2020c, n.p.). With the introduction of GAR, not only that a classification system was established to distinguish between green and brown activities, but also a system to measure banks' engagement in supporting the sustainability-related public goal since GAR computes the percentage of assets on a bank's balance sheet which is Taxonomy-aligned. Additionally, while not directly being targeted to financial institutions, but to its clients, other disclosure regulations of significant importance for an effective bank risk assessment process are NFRD and SFDR.

While the fundamental importance of these regulatory frameworks was acknowledged by various researchers, their shortcomings cannot be overlooked. Regarding the EU Taxonomy, despite it having been placed at the core of regulatory changes that followed, it has been identified that, in its current version, this regulatory framework is rather characterized by high complexity which impedes its practical applicability. Furthermore, the stringent criteria for activities to be considered Taxonomy-compliant narrows significantly the spectrum of projects in scope, a fact that can be recognized by the concerning level of GAR of less than 8% reported by EBA in 2021. Other significant limitations recognized are in terms of data availability and quality. With the soon-to-be enacted SFRD, data will be made available for large corporates only previously in scope of NFRD, which ultimately implies that banks will be required to rely on internally produced or outsourced proxy figures when assessing the risks associated with projects conducted by micro and SME clients. Likewise, to date, only limited attention has been devoted by regulatory bodies to addressing the implementation of ESG risks into risk-management processes of financial institutions. Therefore, given the current minimal progress made in the development of regulatory frameworks to address sustainability considerations from a risk-management perspective, a recalibration of this study's topic was required, and a shift made towards considering ESG risks from a more qualitative, strategy-oriented standpoint.

To deliver on the carbon-reduction commitments by 2050 as established by the EC, academia identified that carbon pricing tends to be somewhat insufficient and amendments in capital requirements might be required to further incentivize banks' commitment to accelerate their contributions toward the green transition. Consequently, the second sub-question of this study aimed at documenting the perceived implications of incorporating sustainability risk factors into capital requirements regulations. The topic's uncertainty and its controversial nature were derived from the contradictory opinions stated among academia. On the one hand, there were advocates of amendments to capital requirements for ESG considerations. For example, Campiglio (2016, pp. 228–229) declares himself in favor of amendments in capital requirements by means of a green relief factor to incentivize banks to accelerate funding green projects. Contrastingly, Baker and Wurgler (2015, p. 315) stress that amendments to capital requirements can have a negative impact as well, particularly by leading to higher banks' cost of capital, if the change results in an increased level, as it would be the case if ESG risks are addressed by means of a penalization system for brown assets. Likewise, Gursoy (2016, p. 72) acknowledged the potential opposite effect of capital requirements amendments, where higher capital requirements will limit the capital available to banks to finance the transition. Zetzsche and Anker-Sørensen (2022, p. 47) as well advocate against capital requirements changes made prematurely considering the sustainability-related development achieved to date. More recently, however, this topic gained nonetheless regulatory and supervisory attention, with EBA having its mandate to assess ESG-related amendments in capital requirements under Pillar I of the Basel Framework due June 2023, for which it published a consultation paper in May 2022 (EBA, 2022a, n.p.). Therefore, it is expected that by mid-2023, the controversy surrounding the topic of the implementation mechanism of ESG factors into capital requirements, as well as the timing of implementation will be respectively addressed.

Coping with the dynamics of the regulatory environment, strategies employed by financial institutions became subject to change as well. This aspect was tackled by the third sub-question addressed in this research, namely *What strategies are employed by credit institutions as a response to newly introduced sustainability risk management regulatory frameworks?* In this regard, academia asserted that while banks tend to approach similar strategic patterns to address sustainability, the prioritization of initiatives and the underlying motives – i.e. environmental, social, and/or business-related motives – allow for establishing a differentiation mechanism between the private sector players (Zimmermann, 2019, p. 2268). Not only that banks have amended the products and services provided to their clients to account for sustainability considerations, but they engaged in conducting ESG initiatives internally such as those related to electrifying office buildings with green energy, decarbonization, and waste management. Likewise, serval dedicated committees and departments were established to tackle the topic at hand. To facilitate the information and knowledge exchange that supports an informed decision-making process for investors, financial institutions conduct as well extensive reporting, disclosing not only their progress towards ESG strategic KPIs but also their compliance with current regulatory requirements by issuing various dedicated reports. Despite the numerous initiatives undertaken by banks in addressing the topic of sustainability, regular bodies tend to express their concerns about the made efforts by the industry, citing EBA's result of the region-wide conducted GAR exercise as mentioned in the paragraphs above.

The last sub-question paving the way toward answering the main research question tackles the extent to which compliance with sustainability-related regulatory requirements can be asserted as a strategic opportunity or, by contrast, a challenge. Academia's focus was placed extensively on quantitative studies researching the relationship between ESG factors and banks' profitability and/or their riskiness. As the number of studies increased, so did the contradictory opinions among them. There are, on the one hand, advocates of the positive impacts ESG has on banks' profitability as determined by, for example, improved market or operational results (Buallay, 2019, p. 110; Miralles-Quirós et al., 2019, pp. 1412–1413). Particularly, some studies identified that, if strategies employed by credit institutions engage all three pillars of ESG, overall positive impacts on all performance metrics, i.e. financial, operational, and market KPIs, can be achieved. Yet, considering the three pillars individually, it appears that E- and G-oriented strategic directions can lead to shareholder value creation. Those studies were, contrastingly, contradicted by other researchers' findings which identified a diminishing return to scale phenomenon, i.e. a convex relationship between ESG strategies and banks' profitability, where profitability experiences a turning point after a certain threshold is reached. Likewise, it was stressed that ESG can be value-destroying to shareholders due to resources being committed to long-term projects with no immediate returns.

Mixed opinions were endorsed with respect to banks' riskiness and their stability. Researchers such as Toth et al. (2021, pp. 441–446) and Gutiérrez-López and Abad-González (2020, p. 2586) identified enhanced liquidity and solvency positions driven by banks' engagement in ESG investments and by providing green products to their clients, where the latter authors, however, mentioned the caveat that improved resilience driven by ESG-linked initiatives holds only in the absence of distressed market conditions. Likewise, a negative relationship between non-performing loans and ESG considerations was further identified, i.e. a lower amount of non-performing loans was achieved by banks which financed projects that supported the green transition. However, it is worth mentioning that banks' size can be a determinant of stability by means of ESG. Namely, it was stressed by academia, that ESG initiatives can enhance banks' stability only if the respective credit institution is of considerable size. For smaller and medium-sized banks, the costs of implementing ESG in their products, services, and operations exceed the generated benefits, resulting in decreased stability positions. Other studies targeted the relationship between ESG and clients' loyalty and trust where positive correlations were recognized. Yet, despite ESG considerations triggering improved loyalty and trust among banks' customers, one could not derive that improved trust will be subsequently reflected in loyalty. Thus, credit institutions need to consider enhancing loyalty and trust individually by means of ESG.

To this end, reflecting upon the main research question of this study, i.e. *What are the perceived strategic implications derived from European sustainability risk management regulatory frameworks for credit institutions?* one could confirm the changes in the banking industry arising from dynamic amendments in the regulatory landscape addressing sustainability. As stated throughout this paper, strategic changes undertaken by financial institutions range from addressing the green demand via providing green products and advisory services to clients undergoing the green transition, to amendments in the governance structure and the implementation of dedicated departments tackling the topic, to conducting initiatives oriented towards ensuring in-house sustainability. Reporting and disclosure were emphasized as mediums of communication and tools for an effective decision-making process, be it targeted at the financial institution itself or its stakeholders. Therefore, it can be stated that sustainability-driven regulatory requirements support the implementation of ESG consideration at an organization-wide level, requiring cross-department involvement, and nevertheless cross-department cooperation and coordination.

The degree to which those regulatory frameworks can be considered a strategic opportunity, or, by contrast, a strategic challenge is a rather controversial topic to date given its novelty and the fact that one could place the related market developments to inception. However, there were both opportunities and challenges identified by academia. Specifically, one of the major strategic opportunities is the ability of banks to drive and to part-take in the transition by providing both financing products and advisory services to their clients. Given the implementation of ESG on a cross-industry level and the cited high volume of financing needs to support the transition to a green economy, enhanced profitability through new sources of revenue is deemed to materialize. By contrast, frameworks' complexities tend to trigger lengthier implementation processes, contradicting the dynamics of change. Furthermore, the lack of data availability and, if available, its questionable quality leads to not only compliance challenges but also operational ones when assessing ESG risks. The limited incentive mechanism in the absence of price models for ESG risks that distinguish between financial institutions committed to the green transformation and their less committed peers has the potential to decelerate the transition process. Yet, as the topic currently undergoes a development process, shortcomings are expected to diminish and be mitigated in the long run.

9 Conclusion

Extreme climatologic events and progressive increases in temperature over the last decades raised numerous concerns regarding the threats future generations are expected to face if no immediate remedial action is taken. It has been identified that approximately 98% of the temperature rise is due to activities people perform daily, of which the main driver is the emission of greenhouse gases. To combat climate change and to subsequently ensure the sustainability of the planet, as well as the long-term well-being of its inhabitants, various geopolitical measures were established where the Paris Agreement can be considered as the fundamental step for global initiatives that followed. Namely, the Paris Agreement called for capping the temperature rise to levels below 2°C, emphasizing the need for cross-national involvement and cooperation to deliver on this public goal. Therefore, on a regional level, aiming at taking a leading position, the European Commission committed itself to making Europe the first climate-neutral continent by mid-century, recognizing the need for both private and public funding to support the transition to a green economy.

It follows that financial institutions, through their funding and lending mechanisms, were expected to become key actors in the transformation, redirecting the capital flow from brown projects to those green, sustainability-aligned ones. Yet, transitioning to a sustainable future implies nevertheless certain challenges and ESG risks emerged, gaining regulatory and supervisory attention due to their systemic nature and leading to amendments in the regulatory landscape. In turn, the banking industry adjusted to ensure compliance with the newly introduced frameworks. In light of the adjusting banking industry, the profitability and riskiness of conducting ESG initiatives became subjects of debate among numerous researchers.

Subsequently, this study aimed at assessing the perceived strategic implications derived from European regulatory frameworks targeting sustainability considerations for credit institutions. Firstly, it has been identified that certain regulatory frameworks are perceived as key drivers of change in the banking industry. Namely, by establishing a classification system for green activities, the EU Taxonomy was gauged as being the fundamental framework driving consequential regulatory amendments. In addition to flagging activities as green as opposed to brown, the green asset ratio has been introduced to measure the percentage of green Taxonomy-aligned assets to banks' total assets, establishing a base through which the engagement of individual financial institutions in delivering the public goal can be judged. In a broader sense, it has been acknowledged that disclosure regulation plays a significant role in communicating the topic's salience, as well as in raising awareness about the need for a cross-industry effort, facilitating nonetheless an informed decision-making process. However, it was determined that the regulatory focus is dedicated to disclosure requirements primarily, with little progress being made in terms of addressing ESG from a quantitative risk-management perspective which led to a recalibration of this work toward perceiving ESG risks implementation in banking processes from a qualitative, strategic viewpoint. Additionally, the topic of amending capital requirements to account for ESG risks triggered other mixed opinions. However, uncertainties in this regard are to be addressed as EBA was commissioned to submit its assessment on amending capital requirements by June 2023.

The dynamics of change in the regulatory environment triggered amendments in banks' strategic directions. The following strategic implication derived from compliance with EU sustainability-related regulatory frameworks are to be listed: introduction of green products and advisory services for clients' transition process, identification and assessment of ESG risks as part of portfolio analysis and decarbonization, as well as amendments in the governance structure, the adherence to various disclosure and reporting requirements and the inclusion of sustainability project targeted to ensure office efficiency. While prioritization of ESG initiatives differed across credit institutions, it can be stated that ESG is a topic that required cross-department engagement, commitment, and coordination.

Therefore, addressing the extent to which sustainability and compliance with sustainability regulatory requirements can be perceived as a strategic opportunity or, contrastingly, a challenge, this research highlighted one more time the contradictory nature of the sustainability topic. Both advantages and disadvantages were acknowledged. While regulatory frameworks facilitate communication and knowledge exchange, the current complexities in frameworks were deemed as decelerating the transition. Similarly, it has been determined that, given the broad nature of the topic affecting various industries, profitability can be facilitated by meeting customers' demand for green products and advisory services. Yet, in the absence of a price mechanism, such as the one derived via a reward or penalizing system for capital requirements, there is no differentiation between market players and thus no regulatory opportunity to gain a competitive advantage by having a greener than the average balance sheet, negatively impacting the incentive of banks to accelerate the transition. Compliance and operational challenges were identified to materialize given the current lack of data and its questionable quality which make banks prone to improperly assessing ESG risks. To address the identified shortcomings, a series of recommendations for improvements can be derived, including increased framework simplicity, the introduction of more incentive mechanisms, acceleration of considering S & G pillars towards achieving full Taxonomy compliance by 2050, as well as addressing the data unavailability by introducing disclosure requirements for SMEs and micro clients. Yet, despite the challenging nature of addressing sustainability and complying with regulatory frameworks, it can be deemed that those challenges are arising from the novelty of the topic and are expected to follow a natural progression towards being mitigated.

On an ending note, while sustainability is a topic of importance and concern, its future path tends to be clouded by severe uncertainties and prone to become subject to political and ideological debates and discourse as a shift is deemed to arise from considering environmental issues only to addressing ESG on its entirety. The prevailing focus placed on combatting climate change at times can be perceived as distracting market players' attention from the other angles of sustainability, i.e. the social and governance pillars. Most market players, be them political figures, regulators, or industry practitioners, appear as having been sidetracked in their efforts to combat environmental concerns from pondering the potential negative externalities of environmental-driven actions on social welfare. It is unquestionable that addressing environmental problems is a first step towards ensuring a sustained well-being for future generations to come; yet, delivering on commitments addressing narrowly the E pillar of ESG cannot be asserted as sufficient and a border consideration of all ESG pillars and their inter-linked nature is desired to occur proactively, where, in addition, both national and regional specifics should be accommodated within the policy-making process. Furthermore, narrowing down the focus to the financial system, due to the high interconnectedness existing between financial actors, delivering on sustainability commitments should not be outsourced to banks only, but should target the other players in the system as well. To be more specific, decisions taken by banks to address sustainability objectives should be contextualized by assessing and evaluating their impact on, for example, the insurance industry and vice versa. Therefore, major complexities arise from the topic of sustainability and are yet to be addressed.

There are several limitations to the study at hand, as well as a series of derived recommendations for future research. Firstly, this study was conducted primarily as a literature review and qualitative content analysis. Therefore, for a better understanding of how sustainability is reflected in the market and perceived by the industry, interviews and surveys with practitioners should be conducted where distinct attention should be provided to the included sample. Secondly, due to the broad nature of the ESG topic and given the fact that it impacts individual departments differently, a focus on certain organizational areas might have uncovered implications that are department specific. As it was highlighted further by academics, banks of different sizes might be impacted differently by ESG considerations and the study at hand did not approach the topic to a greater extent. It follows that future studies can be conducted by focusing on individual geographical regions to uncover region-specific particularities, followed by a comparison study. Given the broader reach of the ESG topic, studies with a narrower focus on a particular department as opposed to an organization-wide view can support bridging the knowledge gap in the existing literature. Nevertheless, following on the previously mentioned proposed area of future research, comparison between departments can be addressed in a different study and certain interlinks identified. Additionally, within individual regional studies, a balanced sample size should be employed, both between the different groups of research partners, i.e. industry practitioners and regulators, and by considering the size of financial institutions included in the research. Comparing the European approach to a different global region could provide insights into how different jurisdictions approach the ESG topic by tracking the progress made to date, as well as deriving certain aspects of "*know-how*" that can be introduced and support the green transformation in regions experiencing implementation barriers. Additionally, due to the high interconnectedness between financial market players, further research should be conducted to evaluate sustainability-related strategic decisions of banking industry players on the other financial system actors.

Abbreviations

AGGI Annual greenhouse gas index
BIS Bank for International Settlements
CO_2 Carbon dioxide
CRD Capital Requirements Directive
CRR Capital Requirements Regulation
CSR Corporate social responsibility
EBA European Banking Authority
EC European Commission
ESA European Supervisory Authorities
ESG Environmental, social and governance
EU European Union
EUR Euro(s)
GAR Green asset ratio
GHG Greenhouse gas
IPCC Intergovernmental Panel on Climate Change
KPIS Key performance indicators
NFRD Non-Financial Reporting Directive
NGFS Network for Greening the Financial System
NOAA National Oceanic and Atmospheric Administration
OECD Organization for Economic Co-operation and Development
ROA Return-on-assets
ROE Return-on-equity
SFDR Sustainable Finance Disclosure Regulation
SMES Small and medium-sized enterprises
SRI Socially responsible investment
UN United Nations
US United States
USD United States dollars
WHO World Health Organization

Notes on Contributor

Alexandra-Cristina Hanganu, MA (2022), Lauder Business School Vienna, recently became an alumnus of the mentioned university, graduating with merits from the study program Strategic Finance & Business Analytics. Her professional interests lie in the areas of environmental, social, governance (ESG), and corporate strategy, currently activating in the field of financial services advisory.

References

Aevoae, G. M., Andrieș, A. M., Ongena, S., & Sprincean, N. (2022). *ESG and Systemic Risk* (Swiss Finance Institute Research Paper Series No. 22–25). Retrieved from https://papers.ssrn.com/sol3/papers.cfm?abstract_id=4058477.

Ahlström, H. (2019). Policy hotspots for sustainability: Changes in the EU regulation of sustainable business and finance. *Sustainability (Switzerland)*, *11*(2), 499–521. https://doi.org/10.3390/su11020499.

Albdiwy, F., Wan Ahmad, W. M., & Abd Sukor, M. E. (2022). Does bank's size affect the relationship between ESG framework and bank's stability? Evidence from the global banking industry. *Journal of Hunan University (Natural Sciences)*, *49*(03), 396–411. https://johuns.net/index.php/publishing/342.pdf.

Alessi, L., Battiston, S., & Melo, A. S. (2021). *Travelling down the green brick road: a status quo assessment of the EU taxonomy*. Retrieved from https://www.ecb.europa.eu/pub/financial-stability/macroprudential-bulletin/html/ecb.mpbu202110_2%7Eea64c9692d.en.html.

Azmi, W., Hassan, M. K., Houston, R., & Karim, M. S. (2021). ESG activities and banking performance: International evidence from emerging economies. *Journal of International Financial Markets, Institutions and Money*, *70*, 1–18. https://doi.org/10.1016/j.intfin.2020.101277.

Bailey, I., & Caprotti, F. (2014). The green economy: Functional domains and theoretical directions of enquiry. *Environment and Planning A*, *46*(8), 1797–1813. https://doi.org/10.1068/a130102p.

Baker, M., & Wurgler, J. (2015). Do strict capital requirements raise the cost of capital? Bank Regulation, Capital Structure, and the Low-Risk Anomaly. *American Economic Review*, *105*(5), 315–320. https://doi.org/10.1257/aer.p20151092.

Bank for International Settlements. (2005). *About BIS – overview*. Retrieved from https://www.bis.org/about/index.htm?m=1001.

Bank for International Settlements. (2017). *Basel III: international regulatory framework for banks*. Retrieved from https://www.bis.org/bcbs/basel3.htm?m=2572.

Bank for International Settlements. (2019). *Basel Framework*. Retrieved from https://www.bis.org/basel_framework/index.htm?m=2697.

Bank for International Settlements. (2021). *Basel Committee consults on principles for the effective management and supervision of climate-related financial risks*. Retrieved from https://www.bis.org/press/p211116.htm.

Bank for International Settlements. (2022). *Principles for the effective management and supervision of climate-related financial risks*. Retrieved from https://www.bis.org/press/p220615.htm.

Bătae, O. M., Dragomir, V. D., & Feleagă, L. (2021). The relationship between environmental, social, and financial performance in the banking sector: A European study. *Journal of Cleaner Production*, *290*, 1–21. https://doi.org/10.1016/j.jclepro.2021.125791.

Ben-Amar, W., Boujenoui, A., & Zéghal, D. (2014). The Relationship between Corporate Strategy and Enterprise Risk Management: Evidence from Canada. *Journal of Management and Strategy*, *5*(1), 1–17. https://doi.org/10.5430/jms.v5n1p1.

Birindelli, G., Dell'Atti, S., Iannuzzi, A. P., & Savioli, M. (2018). Composition and activity of the board of directors: Impact on ESG performance in the banking system. *Sustainability (Switzerland)*, *10*(12), 4699–4719. https://doi.org/10.3390/su10124699.

Breitenfellner, A., Pointner, W., & Schuberth, H. (2019). The Potential Contribution of Central Banks to Green Finance. *Vierteljahrshefte Zur Wirtschaftsforschung*, *88*(2), 55–71. https://doi.org/10.3790/vjh.88.2.55.

Bryman, A., & Bell, E. (2011). *Business Research Methods. 3rd Edition* [Online Reader Vienna]. Retrieved from https://pdfcoffee.com/business-research-methods-3e-pdf drivecom--pdf-free.html.

Buallay, A. (2019). Is sustainability reporting (ESG) associated with performance? Evidence from the European banking sector. *Management of Environmental Quality: An International Journal*, *30*(1), 98–115. https://doi.org/10.1108/MEQ-12-2017-0149.

Buallay, A., Sayed, M., Fadel, J. A., & Shahrokh, S. (2021). Sustainability Reporting and Bank Performance after Financial Crisis. *Competitiveness Review: An International Business Journal*, *31*(4), 747–770. https://doi.org/10.1108/CR-04-2019-0040.

Campiglio, E. (2016). Beyond carbon pricing: The role of banking and monetary policy in financing the transition to a low-carbon economy. *Ecological Economics*, *121*, 220–230. https://doi.org/10.1016/j.ecolecon.2015.03.020.

Carè, R. (2018a). Emerging Practices in Sustainable Banking. In *Sustainable Banking* (pp. 65–92). London: Palgrave Pivot, Cham. https://doi.org/10.1007/978-3-319-73389-0_4.

Carè, R. (2018b). Ethics and Finance: The Unresolved Puzzle. In *Sustainable Banking* (pp. 11–37). London: Palgrave Pivot, Cham. https://doi.org/10.1007/978-3-319-73389-0_2.

Carè, R. (2018c). Exploring the Role of Banks in Sustainable Development. In *Sustainable Banking* (pp. 39–64). London: Palgrave Pivot, Cham. https://doi.org/10.1007/978-3-319-73389-0_3.

Chiaramonte, L., Dreassi, A., Girardone, C., & Piserà, S. (2021). Do ESG Strategies Enhance Bank Stability during Financial Turmoil? Evidence from Europe. *The European Journal of Finance*, 1173–1211. https://doi.org/10.1080/1351847X.2021.1964556.

Climate Bonds Initiative. (2022). *Market Data*. Retrieved from https://www.climatebonds.net/market/data/#issuer-type-charts.

Di Tommaso, C., & Thornton, J. (2020). Do ESG scores effect bank risk taking and value? Evidence from European banks. *Corporate Social Responsibility and Environmental Management*, *27*(5), 2286–2298. https://doi.org/10.1002/csr.1964.

Eliwa, Y., Aboud, A., & Saleh, A. (2021). ESG practices and the cost of debt: Evidence from EU countries. *Critical Perspectives on Accounting*, *79*, 1–27. https://doi.org/10.1016/j.cpa.2019.102097.

El Khoury, R., Nasrallah, N., & Alareeni, B. (2021). ESG and financial performance of banks in the MENAT region: concavity – convexity patterns. *Journal of Sustainable Finance and Investment*, 1–26. https://doi.org/10.1080/20430795.2021.1929807.

European Banking Authority. (2019). *EBA Action Plan on Sustainable Finance*. Retrieved from https://www.eba.europa.eu/sites/default/documents/files/document_library/EBA%20Action%20plan%20on%20sustainable%20finance.pdf.

European Banking Authority. (2021a). *EBA advises the Commission on KPIs for transparency on institutions'*. Retrieved from https://www.eba.europa.eu/eba-advises-commission-kpis-transparency-institutions%E2%80%99-environmentally-sustainable-activities.

European Banking Authority. (2021b). *EBA Report on Management and Supervision of ESG Risks for Credit Institutions and Investment Firms* (EBA Report Series No. 18/2021). Retrieved from https://www.eba.europa.eu/eba-publishes-its-report-management-and-supervision-esg-risks-credit-institutions-and-investment.

European Banking Authority. (2021c). *ESAs propose new rules for taxonomy-related product disclosures*. Retrieved from https://www.eba.europa.eu/esas-propose-new-rules-taxonomy-related-product-disclosures.

European Banking Authority. (2021d). *Mapping climate risk: Main findings from the EU-wide pilot exercise* (EBA Report Series No. 11/2021). Retrieved from https://www.eba.europa.eu/sites/default/documents/files/document_library/Publications/Reports/2021/1001589/Mapping%20Climate%20Risk%20-%20Main%20findings%20from%20the%20EU-wide%20pilot%20exercise%20on%20climate%20risk.pdf.

European Banking Authority. (2022a). *EBA launches discussion on the role of environmental risks in the prudential framework*. Retrieved from https://www.eba.europa.eu/eba-launches-discussion-role-environmental-risks-prudential-framework.

European Banking Authority. (2022b). *EBA publishes binding standards on Pillar 3 disclosures on ESG risks*. Retrieved from https://www.eba.europa.eu/eba-publishes-binding-standards-pillar-3-disclosures-esg-risks.

European Banking Authority. (2022c). *ESAs provide clarifications on key areas of the RTS under SFDR*. Retrieved from https://www.eba.europa.eu/esas-provide-clarifications-key-areas-rts-under-sfdr.

European Banking Authority. (2022d). *Sustainable finance*. Retrieved from https://www.eba.europa.eu/financial-innovation-and-fintech/sustainable-finance.

European Commission. (2020a). *A European Green Deal – Striving to be the first climate neutral continent*. Retrieved from https://ec.europa.eu/info/strategy/priorities-2019-2024/european-green-deal_en.

European Commission. (2020b). *Communication from the Commission to the European Parliament, the Council, the European Economic and Social Committee and the Committee of the Regions – Sustainable Europe Investment Plan – European Green Deal Investment Plan*. Retrieved from https://ec.europa.eu/commission/presscorner/detail/en/fs_20_48.

European Commission. (2020c). *EU taxonomy for sustainable activities*. Retrieved from https://ec.europa.eu/info/business-economy-euro/banking-and-finance/sustainable-finance/eu-taxonomy-sustainable-activities_en.

European Commission. (2020d). *Financing the green transition: The European Green Deal Investment Plan and Just Transition Mechanism*. Retrieved from https://ec.europa.eu/commission/presscorner/detail/en/ip_20_17.

European Commission. (2021). *Causes of climate change*. Retrieved from https://ec.europa.eu/clima/climate-change/causes-climate-change_en.

European Parliament, and the Council. (2020). Regulation (EU) 2020/825 of the European Parliament and of the Council of 18 June 2020 on the establishment of the framework to facilitate sustainable investments, and amending Regulation (EU) 2019/2088. *Official Journal of the European Union*, 1–31. https://eur-lex.europa.eu/legal-content/EN/TXT/?uri=CELEX:32020R0852.

Eurostat. (2021). *Greenhouse gas emission statistics – emission inventories*. Retrieved from https://ec.europa.eu/eurostat/statistics-explained/index.php?title=Greenhouse_gas_emission_statistics_-_emission_inventories.

Gaffney, O., & Steffen, W. (2017). The Anthropocene equation. *The Anthropocene Review*, *4*(1), 53–61. https://doi.org/10.1177/2053019616688022.

Global Sustainable Investment Alliance. (2021). *Global Sustainable Investment Review 2020*. Retrieved from http://www.gsi-alliance.org/wp-content/uploads/2021/08/GSIR-20201.pdf.

Gursoy, O. (2016). Do capital requirements in Basel III Restrict the Financing of Green Economy? A Case Study of a Turkish Bank. In M. M. Erdogdu, A. Y. Mermod, & O. B. A. Yıldırım (Eds.), *Social and Economic Perspectives on Sustainability* (pp. 71–82). London: IJOPEC Publication. Retrieved from https://www.researchgate.net/publication/317598086.

Gutiérrez-López, C., & Abad-González, J. (2020). Sustainability in the banking sector: A predictive model for the European banking union in the aftermath of the financial crisis. *Sustainability (Switzerland)*, *12*(6), 2566–2591. https://doi.org/10.3390/su12062566.

Ibe-enwo, G., Igbudu, N., Garanti, Z., & Popoola, T. (2019). Assessing the relevance of green banking practice on bank loyalty: The mediating effect of green image and bank trust. *Sustainability (Switzerland)*, *11*(17), 1–16. https://doi.org/10.3390/su11174651.

Igbudu, N., Garanti, Z., & Popoola, T. (2018). Enhancing bank loyalty through sustainable banking practices: The mediating effect of corporate image. *Sustainability (Switzerland)*, *10*(11), 4050–4061. https://doi.org/10.3390/su10114050.

Intergovernmental Panel on Climate Change. (2018). *Global Warming of 1.5°C. An IPCC Special Report on the impacts of global warming of 1.5°C above pre-industrial levels and related global greenhouse gas emission pathways, in the context of strengthening the global response to the threat of climate change, sustainable development, and efforts to eradicate poverty*. Retrieved from https://www.ipcc.ch/sr15/.

Intergovernmental Panel on Climate Change. (2021). *Climate Change 2021: The Physical Science Basis – Summary for Policymakers*. Retrieved from https://www.ipcc.ch/report/ar6/wg1/#FullReport.

International Energy Agency. (2021). *Word Energy Outlook 2021*. Retrieved from https://iea.blob.core.windows.net/assets/4ed140c1-c3f3-4fd9-acae-789a4e14a23c/WorldEnergyOutlook2021.pdf.

Lalon, R. M. (2015). Green Banking: Going Green. *International Journal of Economics, Finance and Management Sciences*, *3*(1), 34–42. https://www.sciencepublishinggroup.com/journal/paperinfo.aspx?journalid=173&doi=10.11648/j.ijefm.20150301.15.

La Torre, M., Leo, S., & Panetta, I. C. (2021). Banks and environmental, social and governance drivers: Follow the market or the authorities? *Corporate Social Responsibility and Environmental Management*, 1620–1634. https://doi.org/10.1002/csr.2132.

Llewellyn, D. (1999). *The Economic Rational for Financial Regulation*. Retrieved from https://www.fep.up.pt/disciplinas/pgaf924/PGAF/Texto_2_David_Llewellyn.pdf.

Lucarelli, C., Mazzoli, C., Rancan, M., & Severini, S. (2020). Classification of sustainable activities: EU taxonomy and scientific literature. *Sustainability (Switzerland)*, *12*(16), 6460–6485. https://doi.org/10.3390/su12166460.

Miralles-Quirós, M. M., Miralles-Quirós, J. L., & Hernández, J. R. (2019). ESG performance and shareholder value creation in the banking industry: International differences. *Sustainability (Switzerland)*, *11*(5), 1404–1419. https://doi.org/10.3390/su11051404.

National Oceanic and Atmospheric Administration. (2022a). *State of the Climate: Monthly Global Climate Report for Annual 2021*. National Centers for Environmental Information. Retrieved from https://www.ncei.noaa.gov/access/monitoring/monthly-report/global/202113.

National Oceanic and Atmospheric Association. (2022b). *State of the Climate: Monthly Global Climate Report for April 2022*. National Centers for Environmental Information. Retrieved from https://www.ncei.noaa.gov/access/monitoring/monthly-report/global/202204.

National Oceanic and Atmospheric Administration. (2022c). *The NOAA Annual Greenhouse Gas Index (AGGI)*. NOAA Global Monitoring Laboratory. Retrieved from https://gml.noaa.gov/aggi/aggi.html.

Network for Greening the Financial System. (2021). *NGFS Climate Scenarios for central banks and supervisors*. Retrieved from https://www.ngfs.net/en/ngfs-climate-scenarios-central-banks-and-supervisors.

Newton, D. P., Ongena, S., Xie, R., & Zhao, B. (2022). *Banks vs. Markets: Are Banks More Effective in Facilitating Sustainability?* (Swiss Finance Institute Research Paper No. 22/2022). Retrieved from https://papers.ssrn.com/sol3/papers.cfm?abstract_id=4055293.

Nosratabadi, S., Pinter, G., Mosavi, A., & Semperger, S. (2020). Sustainable Banking; Evaluation of the European Business Models. *Sustainability*, *12*(6), 2314–2333. https://doi.org/10.3390/su12062314.

Och, M. (2020). *Sustainable Finance and the EU Taxonomy Regulation – Hype or Hope?* (Jan Ronse Institute for Company and Financial Law Report Series No. 05/2020). Retrieved from https://papers.ssrn.com/sol3/papers.cfm?abstract_id=3738255.

Organization for Economic Co-operation and Development. (2021). *Climate change in figures*. Retrieved from https://www.oecd.org/environment/cop21-climate-change-in-figures.htm.

Park, H., & Kim, J. D. (2020). Transition towards green banking: role of financial regulators and financial institutions. *Asian Journal of Sustainability and Social Responsibility*, *5*(1), 1–25. https://doi.org/10.1186/s41180-020-00034-3.

Pyka, I., & Nocoń, A. (2021). Banks' capital requirements in terms of implementation of the concept of sustainable finance. *Sustainability (Switzerland)*, *13*(6), 3499–3516. https://doi.org/10.3390/su13063499.

Raworth, K. (2017). A Doughnut for the Anthropocene: humanity's compass in the 21st century. *The Lancet Planetary Health*, *1*(2), 48–49. https://doi.org/10.1016/S2542-5196(17)30028-1.

Schütze, F., & Stede, J. (2020). *EU Sustainable Finance Taxonomy – What Is Its Role on the Road towards Climate Neutrality?* (Deutsches Institut für Wirtschaftsforschung Discussion Paper). Retrieved from https://papers.ssrn.com/sol3/papers.cfm?abstract_id=3749900.

Schütze, F., Stede, J., Blauert, M., & Erdmann, K. (2020). EU taxonomy increasing transparency of sustainable investments. *Deutsches Institut Für Wirtschaftsforschung*, *10*(51), 485–492. https://doi.org/10.18723/diw_dwr:2020-51-1.

Schwartz-Ziv, M. (2017). Gender and Board Activeness: The Role of a Critical Mass. *Journal of Financial and Quantitative Analysis*, *52*(2), 751–780. https://www.cam

bridge.org/core/journals/journal-of-financial-and-quantitative-analysis/article/gender-and-board-activeness-the-role-of-a-critical-mass/29DB15F256ED19CF26DE35F57D24FB14.

Shakil, M. H., Mahmood, N., Tasnia, M., & Munim, Z. H. (2019). Do environmental, social and governance performance affect the financial performance of banks? A cross-country study of emerging market banks. *Management of Environmental Quality: An International Journal, 30*(6), 1331–1344. https://doi.org/10.1108/MEQ-08-2018-0155.

Shakil, M. H., Tasnia, M., & Mostafiz, M. I. (2020). Board gender diversity and environmental, social and governance performance of US banks: moderating role of environmental, social and corporate governance controversies. *International Journal of Bank Marketing, 39*(4), 661–677. https://doi.org/10.1108/IJBM-04-2020-0210.

The Global Commission on the Economy and Climate. (2018). *Unlocking the Inclusive Growth Story of the 21st Century: Accelerating Climate Action in Urgent Times*. Retrieved from https://newclimateeconomy.report/2018/wp-content/uploads/sites/6/2018/09/NCE_2018_FULL-REPORT.pdf.

Toth, B., Lippai-Makra, E., Szladek, D., & Kis, G. D. (2021). The Contribution of ESG Information to the Financial Stability of European Banks. *State Audit Office of Hungary, 66*(3), 429–450. https://ideas.repec.org/a/pfq/journl/v66y2021i3p429-450.html.

United Nations. (2015). *The Paris Agreement*. Retrieved from https://unfccc.int/process-and-meetings/the-paris-agreement/the-paris-agreement.

United Nations. (2021). *Climate Finance*. Retrieved from https://www.un.org/en/climatechange/raising-ambition/climate-finance.

University of Cambridge Institute for Sustainability Leadership. (2014). *Stability and sustainability in Banking Reform – Are environmental risks missing in Basel III?* Retrieved from https://www.unepfi.org/publications/banking-publications/stability-sustainability-in-banking-reform-are-environmental-risks-missing-in-basel-iii-2/.

Valls Martínez, M. C., Cruz Rambaud, S., & Parra Oller, I. M. (2020). Sustainable and conventional banking in Europe. *PLoS ONE, 15*(2), 1–23. https://journals.plos.org/plosone/article?id=10.1371/journal.pone.0229420.

Watts, N., Amann, M., Arnell, N., Ayeb-Karlsson, S., Beagley, J., Belesova, K., Boykoff, M., Byass, P., Cai, W., Campbell-Lendrum, D., Capstick, S., Chambers, J., Coleman, S., Dalin, C., Daly, M., Dasandi, N., Dasgupta, S., Davies, M., di Napoli, C., ... Costello, A. (2021). The 2020 report of The Lancet Countdown on health and climate change: responding to converging crises. *Review, 397*(10269), 129–170. https://doi.org/10.1016/S0140-6736(20)32290-X.

World Bank Group. (2019). *Enabling Private Investment in Climate Adaptation & Resilience – Current Status, Barriers to Investment and Blueprint for Action*. Retrieved from https://openknowledge.worldbank.org/bitstream/handle/10986/35203/Enabling-Private-Investment-in-Climate-Adaptation-and-Resilience-Current-Status-Barriers-to-Investment-and-Blueprint-for-Action.pdf?sequence=5.

World Economic Forum, & Wyman, O. (2021). *Financing the Transition to a Net-Zero Future.* World Economic Forum. Retrieved from https://www.weforum.org/reports/financing-the-transition-to-a-net-zero-future.

World Health Organization. (2019). *Policy briefing: Health and Climate Action.* Retrieved from https://www.euro.who.int/en/health-topics/environment-and-health/Climate-change/publications/2019/sdg-13-health-and-climate-action.

Zetzsche, D. A., & Anker-Sørensen, L. (2022). Regulating Sustainable Finance in the Dark. *European Business Organization Law Review, 23*, 47–85. https://doi.org/10.1007/s40804-021-00237-9.

Zimmermann, S. (2019). Same same but different: How and why banks approach sustainability. *Sustainability (Switzerland), 11*(8), 2267–2287. https://doi.org/10.3390/su11082267.